12-Lead ECGs

A "Pocket Brain"

for

Easy Interpretation

Ken Grauer, MD, F.A.A.F.P.
Professor, Dept. of Community Health & Family Medicine
Assistant Director, Family Practice Residency Program
College of Medicine, University of Florida, Gainesville

Dr. Grauer can be reached by:

Mail — Dr. Ken Grauer
Family Practice Residency Program
625 S.W. 4th Avenue
Gainesville, Florida 32601

Fax — (352) 332-9154
e-Mail — grauer@fpmg.health.ufl.edu
Web site — WWW.KG-EKGPRESS.COM

KG/EKG Press
Gainesville, Florida

KG/EKG Press
Gainesville, Florida

Sole Proprietor— Ken Grauer, MD
Cover Design (and Figures on pages 7, 42, 51)— Kim Battista
Design of *all other* Figures— Ken Grauer, MD
Printing— by Renaissance Printing, Gainesville, Florida

Library of Congress Catalog Card # 98-91365

ISBN # 0-9663389-0-1

00 01 02 / 9 8 7 6 5 4

About the **ECG *"Pocket Brain"***

Electrocardiography is *not* difficult. At least it is not difficult to obtain a basic understanding of the art— and *apply* this understanding to interpretation of the *majority* of 12-lead ECGs and arrhythmias that you will encounter.

The most difficult part of electrocardiography is learning (and then *remembering*) the various criteria used to diagnose complex ECG findings such as left ventricular hypertrophy and bundle branch block. Practically speaking, however— ***there is much less to learn*** (and memorize) ***than most people think***. Herein lies the *secret* of the ECG *Pocket* Brain: it facilitates understanding of basic ECG concepts and *lightens* the "memory load"— by providing *ready* recall of those *KEY* facts and figures needed for successful 12-lead interpretation.

How to Use the Pocket Brain

We suggest you first familiarize yourself with the contents of the **ECG *Pocket* Brain**. After doing so— we encourage you to carry it with you in your daily practice. Refer to it *whenever* you encounter an ECG about which you have a question. Doing so should not only eliminate the need to memorize cumbersome tables and ciriteria— but also facilitate and improve your ECG interpretation ability, while at the same time making the process much more enjoyable.

A *KEY* feature of the *Pocket* Brain is the ***Rapid Find* Contents** (*inside* front cover)— which allows you to locate (within seconds!) *whatever* concepts or topics you are searching for. Specific page referrals facilitate speed in finding information.

— *Other Material by this Author* —

- Grauer K: **12-Lead ECG: *Practice Exercises* *with* *Explained Answers***— 1999. Price = $10, by **KG/EKG Press** (an excellent companion *practice guide* to go with the ECG *Pocket* Brain book).

- ❖ Grauer K: ***The Pocket Brain: Arrhythmia Management*** *and* ***Cardiac Arrest***— July, 1998. Price = $10, by **KG/EKG Press** (to be updated soon).
  - Grauer K: **Cardiac Arrest: *Practice*** *in* ***Running*** *a* ***Code*** — 1999. Price = $10, by **KG/EKG Press**.

- ❖ Grauer K: *A* ***Pocket Brain*** *on* ***ETT*** *(Exercise Treadmill Testing)*— 1999. Price = $10, by **KG/EKG Press**.
  - Grauer K: ***ETT Case Studies*** *(with* ***Explained Answers)*** — 2000. Price = $10, by **KG/EKG Press**.

- ❖ Grauer K: ***A Practical Guide to ECG Interpretation***- 2th Edition (Mosby Lifeline- 1998, 500 pages) — Book code #32123 — $34.95 — To order, please call **Mosby/Harcourt Brace** (1-800 325-4177).

Starting Out: *Review of* ***The Basics***

The *KEY* to interpretation of *any* ECG is to utilize a ***Systematic* Approach**. The approach we suggest for interpreting each 12-lead ECG that you encounter entails *systematic* assessment of each of the following:

- **R** ate
- **R** hythm
- **I** ntervals (PR/QRS/QT)

- **A** xis
- **H** ypertrophy
- **I** nfarct (*QRST changes*)

We outline key elements to assess for each of the above parameters on the ***Inside Back* Cover** of this ECG *Pocket* Brain. Discussion is limited here to the following points:

- The **purpose** of having (and *regularly* using) a systematic approach is simple: It ***prevents*** you from ***overlooking*** potentially important findings.
- Additional benefits include increased **accuracy**, improved organization, and surprisingly— *increased* ***speed*** in completing your interpretation.

The process of 12-lead ECG interpretation should be thought of as consisting of ***two* major steps**: 1) Descriptive analysis; and 2) The clinical impression.

> ❖ **KEY Clinical Point**— The secret of successful ECG interpretation depends on keeping these 2 steps *separate* in your mind:

- Step #1 = ***Descriptive* Analysis**— is accomplished first: Simply *describe* what is seen on the tracing (as per the checklist review that we outline on the *Inside Back Cover*). Ideally— *WRITE OUT* your findings.
- Step #2 = The ***Clinical* Impression**— should only come *after* Step #1 has been completed. Those *specific* findings identified in descriptive analysis should *now* be interpreted *in light of* the clinical context (i.e., as defined by the patient's age, presenting complaint, and additional relevant clinical history).

Why 2 separate steps? Consider the following:

Symmetric T wave inversion is often seen in the *anterior* leads (V_1, V_2, and V_3) of pediatric patients. In an otherwise healthy child (with no heart murmur) — this finding represents a completely *benign* normal variant (commonly referred to as a ***Juvenile* T Wave Pattern**). However, the *same* ECG (with *identical* T wave inversion) would have to be interpreted very *differently* IF the patient in question was an *older* adult with *new-onset* chest pain (in whom this finding should strongly suggest ischemia). Descriptive analysis is the *same* in both cases (i.e., "symmetric T wave inversion in leads V_{1-3}") — but the clinical impression is *very* different!

Tips for ***Applying*** the ***Systematic*** **Approach**

In the process of *regularly* using the *Systematic Approach* (that is outlined on the ***Inside Back* Cover**) — consider the following:

- Be sure to carefully **survey *all*** 12 **leads** on the ECG— *except* perhaps for lead aVR (which can usually be ignored *unless* you suspect dextrocardia or lead mis-placement— *See below*).
- Always assess *Intervals* at an *early* point in the process! If the rhythm is sinus and the QRS complex is wide, determine ***WHY*** the **QRS** is **Wide** — *before* going further (RBBB? LBBB? IVCD? — *See page 21*).
- Remember the concept of "***patterns** of **leads***". For example, when looking at lead **I** — look at lead **aVL** at the *same* time (since *both* leads view a similar area of the heart). When looking at lead **III**— look also at leads **II** and **aVF** (the other inferior leads- *See page 50*). With time, your experienced eye learns to *simultaneously* assess the two or three leads in each **lead group** (*page 43*).

❖ **Lead Reversal** (or dextrocardia) should be suspected— IF there is: 1) **global *negativity*** in lead **I** (negative P wave, QRS complex *and* T wave); 2) an ***upright* QRS** complex in lead **aVR**; *and/or* 3) a ***negative* P** wave in lead **II**.

Dextrocardia is much *less* common than lead reversal. Suspect it if R wave progression is *reversed* (and if you hear heart sounds on the right!).

Rate & Rhythm

Rhythm Analysis: *Assessing the 5 Parameters*

The most important clinical point (and the *real KEY* to rhythm interpretation) is to utilize a ***systematic* approach.** The system we favor is based on assessing for the following 5 parameters:

- ***P*** waves **?**
- ***QRS*** width **?**
- **R** *egular* rhythm **?**
- Are P waves **R** *elated* to the QRS **?**
- Heart **R** *ate* **?**

❖ **Memory Aid**: *"Watch your **P**'s and **Q**'s — and the 3 **R**'s".*

Heart Rate: *Calculating the Rate*

The easiest way to estimate heart rate is to use the *"Rule of 300"* :

> ❖ The ***"Rule of 300"*** — Provided that the rhythm is regular, heart rate can be *estimated* by dividing 300 by the number of large boxes in the R-R interval (*See page 5*).

With the ECG machine set at the standard recording speed of 25 mm/second— the time required to record each ***little* box** on ECG grid paper is **0.04 second.** (Vertically, each little box is 1 mm in amplitude.)

The time required to record each ***large* box** on ECG grid paper is **0.20 second** (because there are 5 little boxes in each large box, and 5 **X** 0.04 = 0.20).

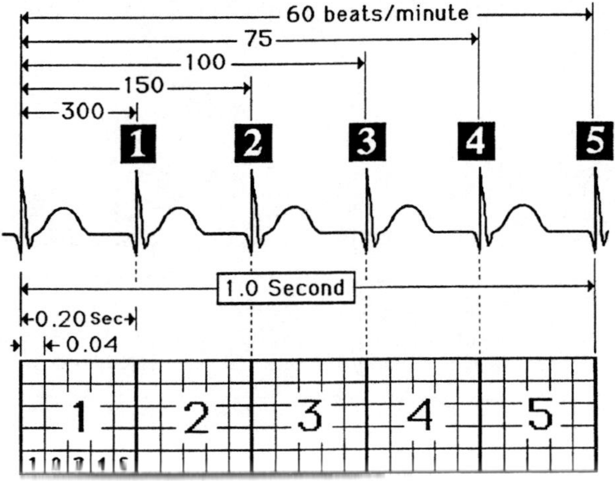

It can therefore be seen (*from the Figure*) that the time required to record **5 *large* boxes** will be one *full* second (0.20 X 5 = **1.0 second**). Thus, if a QRS complex occurs each large box (as in this Figure) — then the R-R interval will be 0.20 second, and the ***rate*** of the rhythm is **300 beats/minute** (i.e., 5 beats occur each second **X** 60 seconds/minute = 300/minute).

We schematically show in the Figure above that IF the R-R interval is **2** large boxes— then the rate will be 300 ÷ 2 = **150** beats/minute;

- if the R-R is **3** boxes, the rate will be **100**/min (300 ÷ 3)
- if the R-R is **4** boxes, the rate will be **75**/min (300 ÷ 4),
  - and so on . . .

Sinus Mechanism Rhythms/Arrhythmias

By definition, the **P wave** will always be ***upright*** in standard **lead II** when the mechanism of the rhythm is sinus.

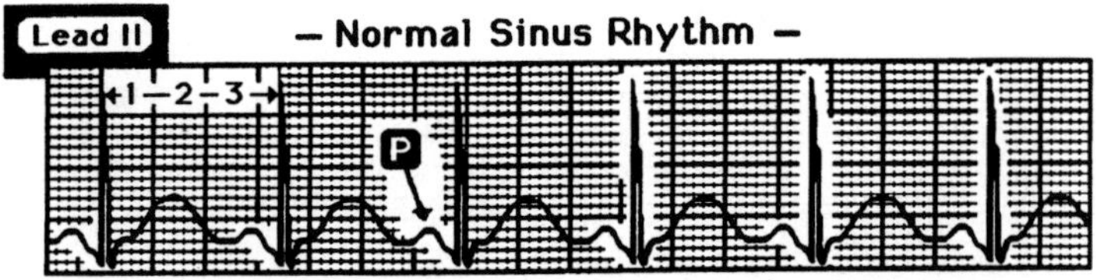

<u>KEY Clinical Point</u>— <u>IF</u> the P wave in lead II is *not* upright— then sinus rhythm is *not* present (*unless* there is dextrocardia or lead reversal).

By the ***Rule of 300*** — the rate of the sinus rhythm shown above is ≈ 85 beats/minute (since the R-R interval is between 3 and 4 large boxes, or between 100 and 75 beats/minute— *as per the Figure on page 5*).

There are four basic types of sinus mechanism rhythms:

- ***Normal* sinus rhythm (NSR)** — regular rhythm; rate *between* 60-99 beats/minute.
- **Sinus *bradycardia*—** regular rhythm; rate *below* 60 beats/minute.
- **Sinus *tachycardia*—** regular rhythm; rate 100 beats/minute or *faster* in an adult patient.
- **Sinus *arrhythmia*—** *irregular* rhythm <u>*despite*</u> the presence of a sinus mechanism. Sinus arrhythmia is a common *normal* variant that is frequently seen in otherwise healthy children and young adults.

Other Supraventricular (⇒ *Narrow QRS*) Arrhythmias

A *supraventricular* rhythm is defined to be one in which the electrical impulse originates <u>*at*</u> or <u>*above*</u> the AV node (i.e., at or above the double *dotted* line below).

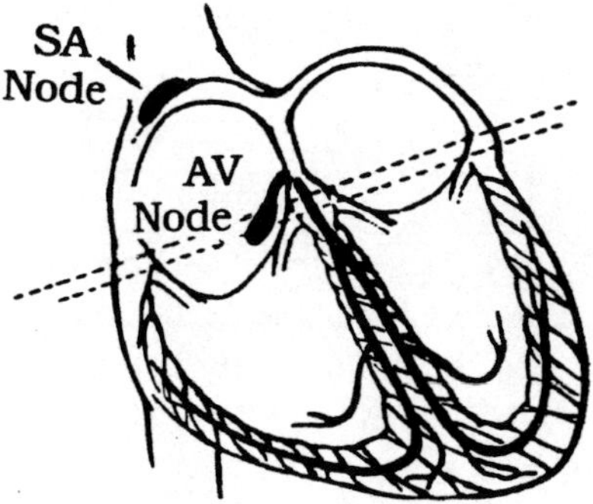

In addition to the sinus mechanism rhythms (that were just described) — the ***other*** principal **entities** in this category include:

1. Atrial fibrillation
2. Atrial flutter
3. PSVT (paroxysmal supraventricular tachycardia)
4. Junctional (AV nodal) rhythms

Atrial Fibrillation (A Fib)

Atrial fibrillation is characterized by the presence of an ***irregularly* irregular** rhythm in the absence of P waves. Undulations in the baseline (known as "fib waves") may sometimes be seen.

A Fib is therefore described as having:

- a ***rapid*** **ventricular response**— if the rate averages *over* 120 beats/minute.
- a ***controlled*** (*moderate*) **ventricular response**— if the rate averages *between* ≈70-110 beats/minute.
- a ***slow*** **ventricular response**— if the rate averages *less* than 60 beats/minute.

Lead II A Fib– with a **controlled** ventricular response

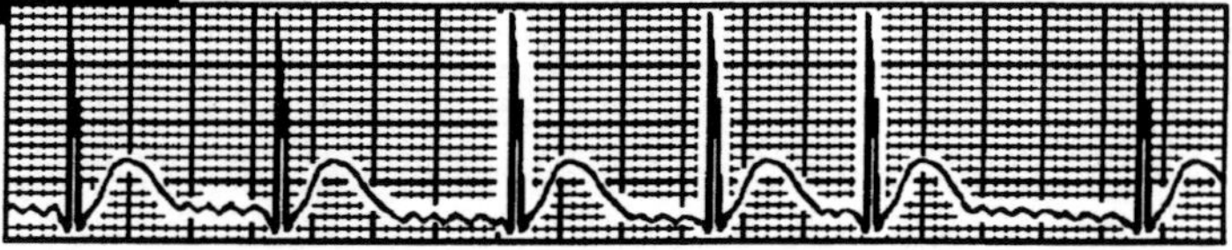

(Note– moderately coarse "**fib waves**")

MAT (*Multifocal Atrial Tachycardia*)

A Fib should be distinguished from ***MAT***— in which the rhythm is also irregularly irregular, but in which definite P waves *are* present (*See below*). Clinically, MAT is most often seen in patients with either pulmonary disease or multisystem problems (sepsis, shock, electrolyte abnormalities, etc.). *Treat the underlying cause!*

Lead II MAT– with multiple different P waves

Atrial Flutter (A Flutter)

Atrial flutter is characterized by a special pattern of *regular* atrial activity that in adults *almost always* (and almost *magically*) occurs at a rate of **300/minute**. Atrial flutter typically manifests a ***sawtooth*** appearance that is usually best seen in the inferior leads— although at times, flutter waves may be *very* subtle (*arrows below*).

- The ***most* common** ventricular response to atrial flutter (*by far!*) is with **2:1 AV conduction**. This means that the ventricular rate with *untreated* atrial flutter is usually *close* to **150/min** (i.e., ≈300 ÷ 2).
- Less commonly with flutter there is **4:1** AV conduction (vent. rate ≈75/minute)— or a ***variable*** (= irregular) ventricular response. *Odd conduction ratios* (i.e., 1:1, 3:1, 5:1) *are rare*. Note how much easier it is to identify flutter with 4:1 conduction (*lower tracing*).

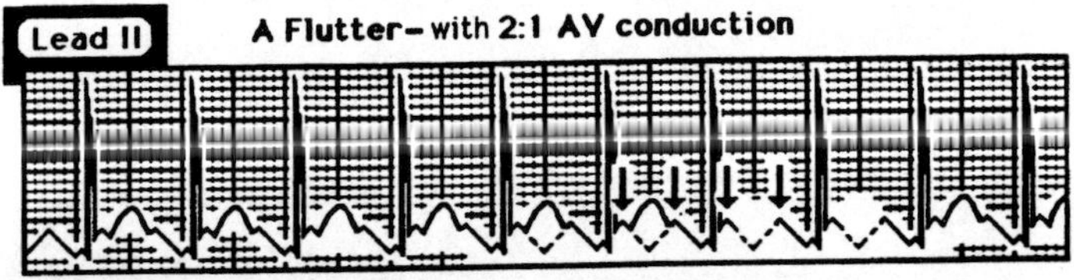

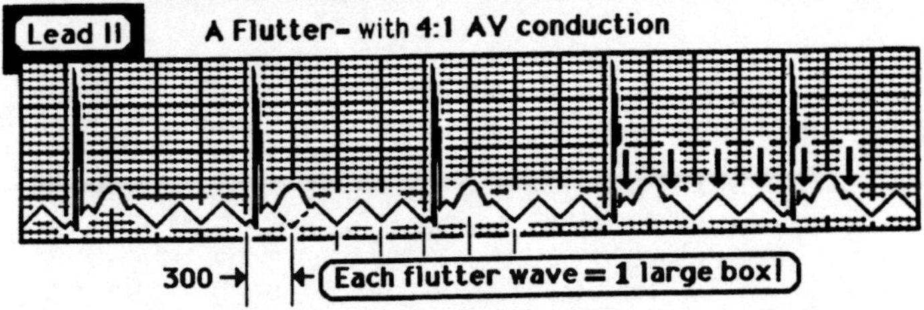

PSVT (<u>P</u>aroxysmal <u>S</u>upra<u>V</u>entricular <u>T</u>achycardia)

PSVT is a regular *supraventricular* tachycardia that most often occurs at a rate of between 150 to 240 beats/minute (*See Figure*). Atrial activity is usually *not* evident— although subtle notching or a negative deflection (representing *retrograde* atrial activity) may sometimes be seen at the tail end of the QRS complex.

Formerly this rhythm was known as PAT or PJT (paroxysmal atrial or junctional tachycardia). Mechanistically, **PSVT** is a *reentry* tachycardia that almost always involves the AV node (ergo the most recent name for this rhythm which is **AVNRT** = ***<u>AV</u> <u>N</u>odal <u>R</u>eentry <u>T</u>achycardia***). The impulse *continues* to circulate *within* the AV node *until* the reentry pathway is interrupted (by drugs, vagal maneuvers— or stops spontaneously).

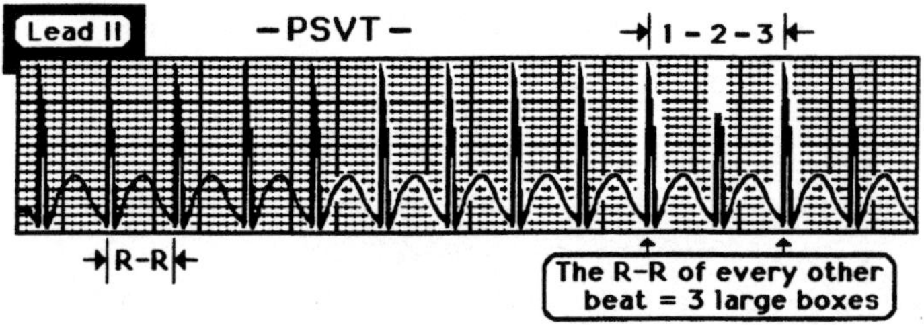

❖ ***<u>KEY</u>***- Accurate determination of heart rate is essential for assessment of the SVTs (*See page 17*). When the rhythm is regular and the rate is fast (*as above*) — calculating the rate is most easily accomplished using the ***"Every-other-Beat"* Method** (i.e., the R-R interval of every *other* beat in the above tracing is 3 large boxes— so that *half* the rate ≈100/minute. This means that the *actual* rate must be *twice* this (≈ **200/min** in the above tracing).

Vagal Manuevers

Vagal maneuvers are commonly used to facilitate ECG diagnosis— *and/or* to treat certain cardiac arrhythmias. Vagal maneuvers work by producing a *transient* increase in parasympathetic tone— thus *slowing* conduction through the AV node.

- *Carotid Sinus Massage* (**CSM**) — Always perform under *constant* ECG monitoring. Use the *right* carotid first. *Never* press on both carotids at the same time. Remember that the carotid sinus is located *high* in the neck (at the angle of the jaw!). Warn patient that the maneuver will be uncomfortable (as very *firm* pressure is needed for success). Rub for no more than 3-5 seconds at a time. If no response— may repeat CSM on the *left* side and/or after giving medication. *Don't* do CSM if patient has a carotid bruit (as you may dislodge a plaque!).
- ***Valsalva***— Have patient forcibly exhale (*bear down*) against a closed glottis (*as if trying to go to the bathroom*) for up to 15 seconds at a time. If properly performed— may be even more effective than CSM! Patient should be *supine* when attempting Valsalva.

Usual Response to ***Vagal* Maneuvers**

- **Sinus Tachycardia**— *gradual slowing* to CSM (with *resumption* of tachycardia on release of pressure).
- **PSVT**— responds with either abrupt *termination* of PSVT (and conversion to sinus rhythm) — or there is *no response* at all.
- **Atrial Fib** or **Flutter**— CSM typically *slows* the ventricular rate (which may facilitate rhythm diagnosis).
- **Ventricular Tachycardia**— does *not* respond to CSM.

Junctional (*AV Nodal*) Rhythms

Junctional (or AV Nodal) rhythms are regular supraventricular rhythms in which atrial activity reflects an AV nodal site of origin. As a result, the **P wave** in **lead II** with a junctional rhythm will *either* be ***negative*** (preceding or following the QRS) — **or *absent*** completely. There are three basic types of junctional rhythms (with the type determined by the *rate* of the rhythm):

- **AV nodal *escape* rhythm—** when the junctional rate in an *adult* is between 40-60 beats/minute (and the rhythm arises because the SA node is either delayed or *fails* in its pacemaking function) — *See below.*
- ***Accelerated* junctional rhythm—** when the junctional rate speeds up to between 61-99 beats/minute and *takes over.* the pacemaking function.
- **Junctional *tachycardia*—** when the rate *exceeds* 100/minute.

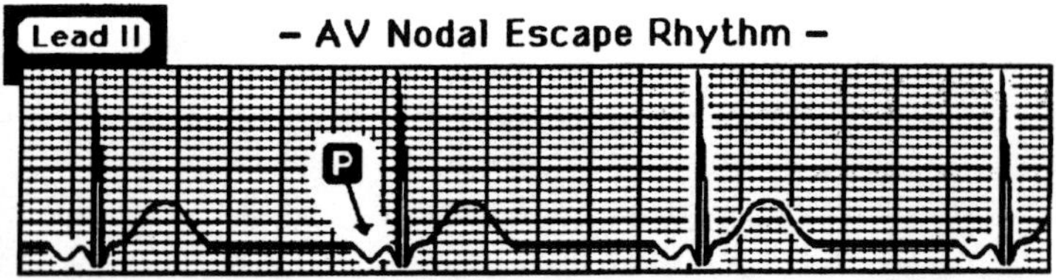

(Negative P in lead II; narrow QRS; rate between 40-60/min)

> ***KEY* Clinical Point**- In adults, the rate of an AV nodal *escape* rhythm is normally between **40-60 beats/minute**. If the rate is *faster* than this and the patient is taking digoxin— *Strongly suspect* ***digitalis* toxicity.**

Premature Beats

Premature beats are QRS complexes that interrupt the underlying rhythm by occurring ***earlier*** than expected. They are of 3 basic types (*See Figure below*):

- **PACs** (Premature *Atrial* Contractions) — when the underlying rhythm is interrupted by an early beat arising from somewhere in the *atria* other than the SA node (*different* shape P Wave— *See Figure below*). Most often the impulse will be conducted with a *narrow* QRS complex that is *identical* in appearance to that of normal sinus-conducted beats.
- **PJCs** (Premature *Junctional* Contractions) — when the underlying rhythm is interrupted by an early beat arising from the *AV node* or *junction*. Most often the impulse is conducted with a narrow QRS complex that is *similar* (or identical) in appearance to that of normal sinus-conducted beats. The P wave in lead II is negative or absent (*See below*).
- **PVCs** (Premature *Ventricular* Contractions) — when the underlying rhythm is interrupted by an early beat arising from the *ventricles*. PVCs are *wide* and have an appearance that is *very* different from that of the normal sinus-conducted beats.

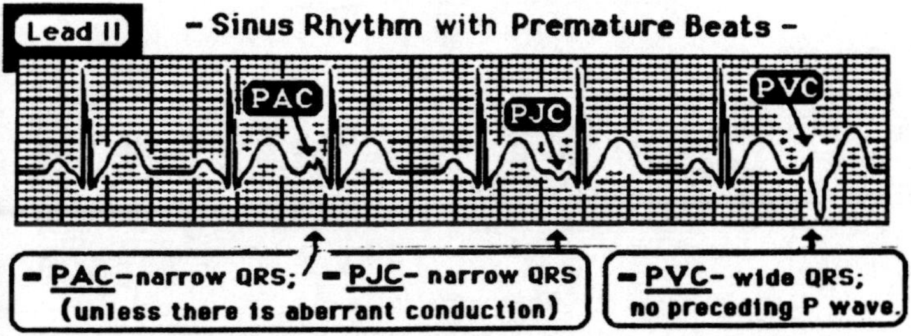

Blocked PACs and ***Aberrant*** **Conduction**

Although most premature *supraventricular* beats (PACs or PJCs) are conducted to the ventricles *normally* (i.e., with a *narrow* QRS complex) — this is *not* always the case. Instead, PACs (or PJCs) may sometimes occur so early in the cycle as to be **"blocked"** (i.e., *non-conducted*) — because the conduction system is still in an *absolute* refractory state. At other times, *premature* beats may occur during the *relative* refractory period— in which case ***aberrant* conduction** (with a *widened* QRS) occurs. Practically speaking, aberrant conduction is most likely to take the form of *some* type of bundle branch block/hemiblock pattern (most commonly RBBB). Attention to **QRS *morphology*** may help to distinguish between aberrancy and ventricular beats (*See page 15*).

> **KEY Clinical Point**- Blocked PACs are often *subtle* and difficult to detect. They *will* be found if looked for— they'll often be hiding (notching) a part of the *preceding* T wave (See *subtle* T wave *notching* in the Figure below).

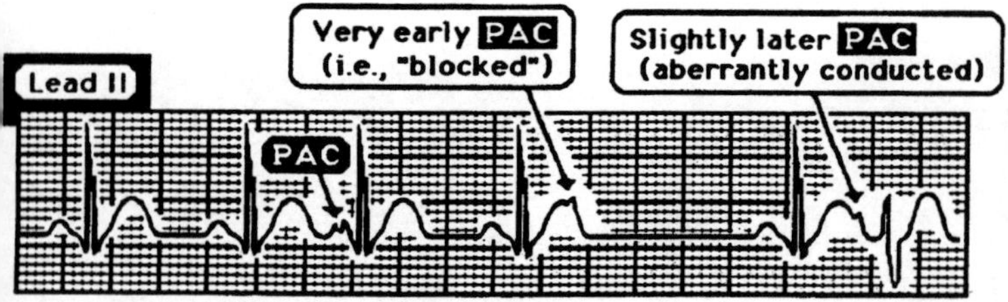

- Sinus Rhythm with PACs -

❖ **<u>QRS Morphology</u>**— To help assess the etiology of wide beats *when the QRS complex is* ***upright*** *in* V_1.

	Suggests a SUPRAVentricular Etiology/Aberration	Of NO HELP in Differentiation	Suggests a VENTricular Etiology
RIGHT-sided leads (V_1, MCL_1)	**Lead V_1** Taller RIGHT rabbit ear 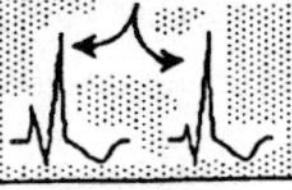	No S wave (or S doesn't descend to baseline) 	Taller LEFT rabbit ear 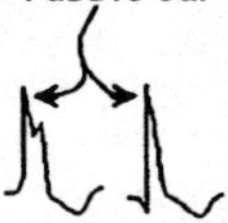
LEFT-sided leads (I, V_5, V_6, MCL_6)	Wide terminal S wave 	R wave is about equal to S wave 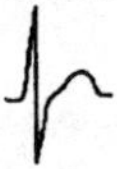	Totally (or almost so) negative QRS 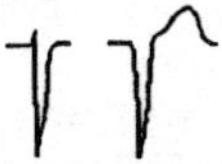

❖ **<u>QRS Morphology</u>**— To help assess the etiology of wide beats *when the QRS complex is* ***negative*** *in* V_1.

	Consistent with a SUPRAVentricular Etiology/Aberration	Suggests a VENTricular Etiology	
RIGHT-sided leads (V_1, MCL_1)	S wave has steep downslope 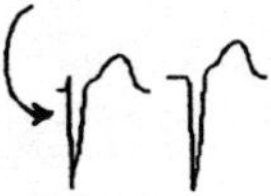	**Lead V_1** Fat initial r wave 	Slurring of downslope 
LEFT-sided leads (I, V_5, V_6, MCL_6)	Completely upright complex 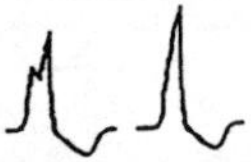	q in V_6 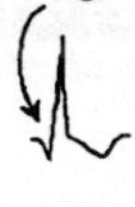	Negative QRS complex 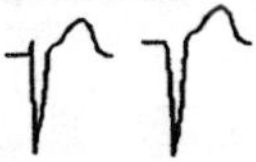

Sustained Ventricular (⇒ Wide QRS) Arrhythmias

With the exception of the chaotic variability of ventricular fibrillation— the *sustained* ventricular rhythms are most often regular (or at least fairly regular) rhythms that originate from a site in the ventricles. As a result of their ventricular origin, the QRS complex is wide and very different in appearance from that of normal sinus-conducted beats.

Ventricular rhythms may arise either as ***escape*** rhythms (if supraventricular pacemakers fail) — or ***usurping* rhythms** (when the ventricular focus accelerates and *takes over* the pacemaking function from the preexisting supraventricular pacemaker). Atrial activity with the ventricular rhythms may be absent, unrelated to the QRS complex, or retrograde.

- ***Slow* Idioventricular *escape* rhythm**— when the ventricular rate is *"slow"* (i.e., between 20-40 beats/minute— which is the usual rate range of an intrinsic ventricular escape focus).
- **AIVR (*Accelerated* IdioVentricular Rhythm)** — when the rate is *more than* 40/min) — *but does NOT exceed* 110-120 beats/minute (*See Figure below*).
- **Ventricular tachycardia (VT)** — when the rate exceeds 120-130/minute. VT is *always* a usurping rhythm (*See page 18*).

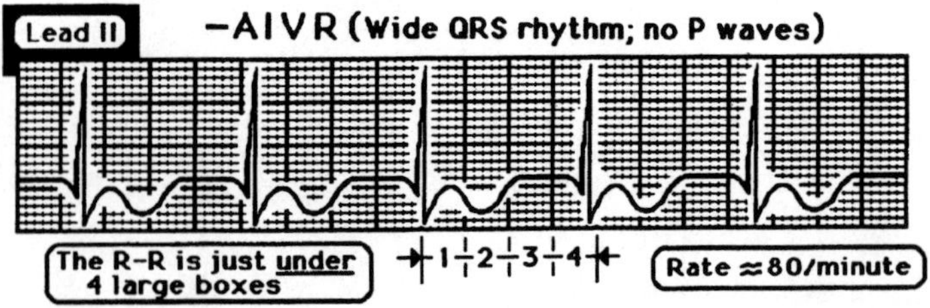

2 ***KEY*** **"Lists"** for Interpretating ***Tachycardias***

The **1st priority** in evaluating *any* tachycardia is to ensure that the patient is ***hemodynamically* stable.** If not— *immediately* cardiovert! If the patient is unstable, it *no longer matters* what the rhythm may be (i.e., VT or SVT with aberrant conduction) — since the need for *immediate* synchronized cardioversion will be the same.

However, IF the patient *is STABLE* hemodynamically — an attempt *can* be made to determine the etiology of the tachycardia *before* proceding further. IF the QRS is ***NARROW*** (in *all* 12 leads!)— then the rhythm is an **"SVT"** (*SupraVentricular* Tachycardia):

Common Causes of a ***Regular*** **SVT**
(*without* sign of atrial activity)

1. Sinus Tachycardia
2. Atrial Flutter
3. PSVT

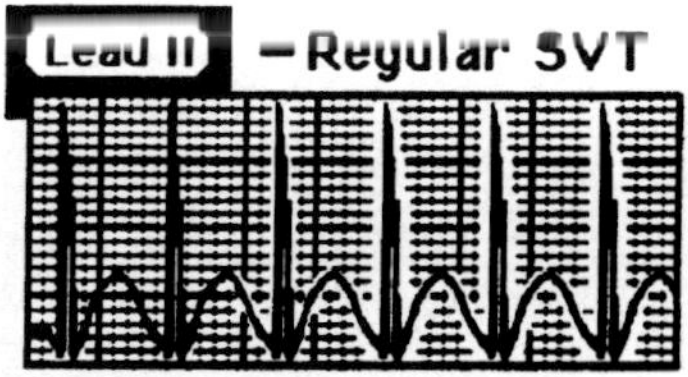

To distinguish between the above 3 entities, look at the rate: **Sinus tachycardia** *rarely* exceeds 150/minute in an adult patient. **Atrial flutter** most often conducts at a ventricular rate *close* to **150**/min (*See page 9*). ***A Fib** is ruled out if the rhythm is regular.* Use of a **vagal maneuver** (*page 11*) — and/or obtaining a 12-lead ECG *during* the tachycardia may help to determine the cause.

IF the QRS is ***WIDE***— then the rhythm is a ***WCT*** (*Wide-Complex* Tachycardia). Once again the *first* priority is to determine if the patient is ***hemodynamically*** **stable**. If not— *cardiovert* ! But IF the patient with WCT *is STABLE*— Consider the possible causes (*See below*):

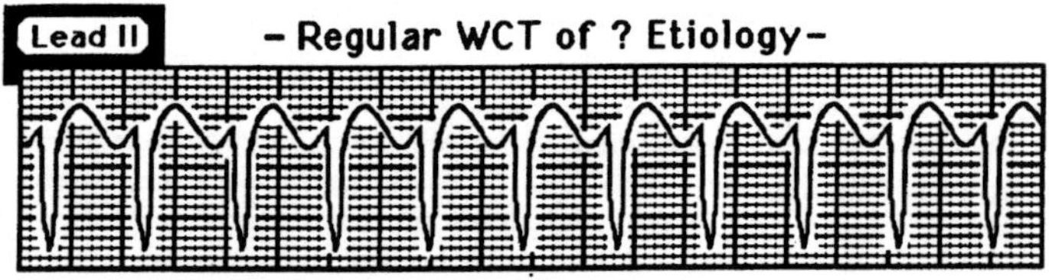

Common Causes of a Regular, ***W****ide-**C**omplex* **T**achycardia (***WCT***) of *Uncertain* Etiology

---

1. *Ventricular Tachycardia* (**VT**)
2. VT (especially if patient *older* and *has* heart disease)
— Causes ***#3*** *through* *#8* — **VT/VT/VT** !!!!!

9. SVT with *pre-existing* bundle branch block
10. SVT with *aberrant* conduction

❖ ***KEY Points*** — Always ***assume*** **VT** (until *proven* otherwise!) Treat the patient accordingly. Obtaining a 12-lead ECG *during* the tachycardia may help with diagnosis. Pay special attention to **QRS morphology** in leads V_1 and V_6 (*See page 15*) — and to **axis** (*marked* LAD or RAD *during* the tachycardia suggests VT). Compare QRS morphology of the WCT with *prior* tracings (if available). Remember— some patients with VT may remain awake and alert for *long* periods of time!

The PR Interval

As shown in the Figure below— the ***PR interval*** is defined as the period that extends from the *onset* of atrial depolarization (beginning of the P wave) — until the onset of *ventricular depolarization* (beginning of the QRS complex).

The best lead to use for measuring the PR interval is **lead II**. In adults, if the P wave is *upright* in this lead (i.e., if there is sinus mechanism) — the PR interval is considered **normal** if *between* **0.12** and **0.20 second**. The PR is "short" if it is *less* than 0.12 second in lead II (as may occur with WPW when the AV node is bypassed — *See page 27*). The PR is long if *more* than 0.20 second (i.e., if clearly *more* than a *LARGE* box in duration).

<u>**Note**</u>- The *isolated* finding of **1° AV block** (in the *absence* of other cardiac pathology) has virtually no clinical significance (and no effect on long-term outcome) — even if the PR interval is very long.

Precise determination of a PR interval that falls within the normal range is *not* necessary. Clinically in this situation— it suffices to say that the PR interval is "normal".

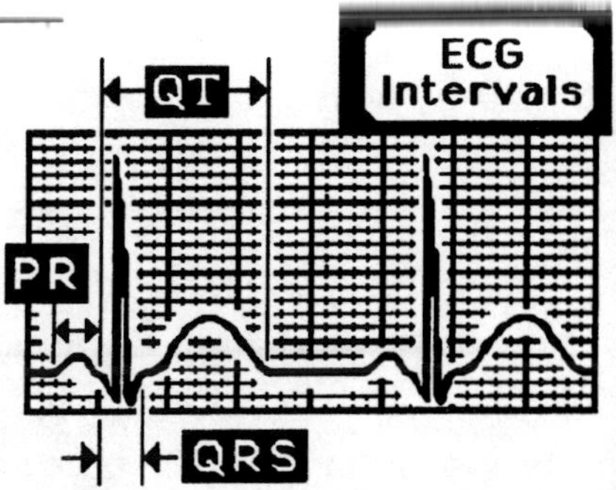

The QRS Interval/Bundle Branch Block

The ***QRS interval*** represents the time it takes for ventricular depolarization to occur. With sinus rhythm in adults— the process of ventricular activation should **normally** be complete in ***no more*** than **0.10 second**. Key points to keep in mind are that:

- QRS duration can be measured from *any* of the 12 leads of a standard ECG. **Select** the **lead *in which*** the **QRS** complex **appears** to be ***longest***.
- Practically speaking— all that matters is whether the QRS is normal or wide. Precise measurement of QRS duration for a complex that is clearly *within* the normal range is *not* necessary.
- Given that 0.10 second is the upper normal limit for QRS duration in adults— the QRS complex is said to be ***WIDE*** if it is <u>**more**</u> than ***HALF*** a ***large* box** in duration.
- These limits do *not* hold true for children (for whom *lesser* degrees of QRS prolongation are abnormal).

If the ***QRS Complex*** *is* ***Wide***

❖ <u>IF</u> the rhythm is *supraventricular* and the QRS complex is *WIDE*— we suggest you ***short-circuit*** your systematic approach. Instead— *immediately* branch to the algorithm shown on page 21:

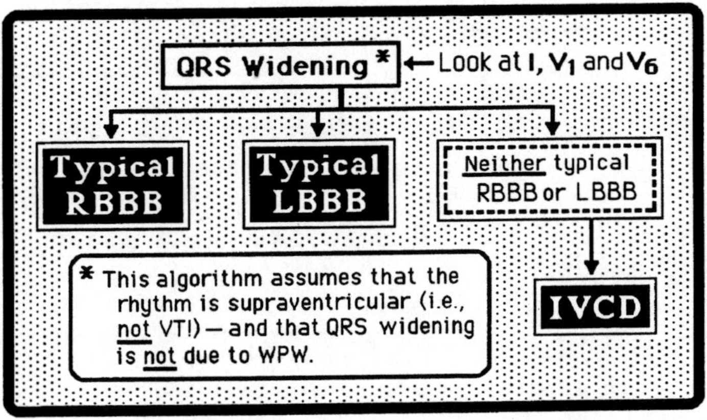

❖ Thus, IF the QRS is wide— determine ***WHY*** it is **wide** *before* proceding further with your interpretation. Practically speaking— there are *only* 3 possibilities: *

- Possibility #1- There may be ***typical* RBBB** (Right Bundle Branch Block)
- Possibility #2- There may be ***typical* LBBB** (*Left Bundle Branch Block*).
- Possibility #3- The QRS complex is wide- but *neither* typical RBBB *nor* typical LBBB is present. In this case, the reason for QRS widening must be the presence of **IVCD** (*IntraVentricular Conduction Delay*).

Note- The 3 ***KEY* leads** (and the *only* 3 leads needed) to determine the *type* of conduction defect (RBBB, LBBB, or IVCD)- are **leads I, V_1**, and **V_6**.

❖ Typical RBBB

The appearance of *typical* complete RBBB in the three *KEY* leads (I, V_1, and V_6) is schematically shown in the Figure below. Diagnostic criteria include:

- **QRS widening** to *at least* **0.11 second**. (There is *incomplete* RBBB if morphology is typical but the QRS is *not* prolonged to at least 0.11 second.)
- An **rSR'** or **rsR'** in *right-sided* **lead V_1**.
- A ***wide*** **terminal S wave** in **leads I** and **V_6**. The QRS is usually predominantly positive in these *left-sided* leads with RBBB. There may or may not be an initial small q wave. The *KEY* to the diagnosis of RBBB is the *wide terminal S wave* in these leads.

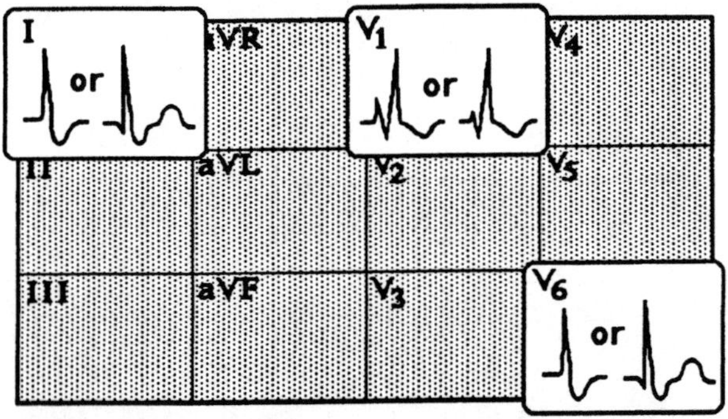

ECG appearance of the QRS complex in the 3 *KEY* leads with *typical* **complete RBBB**. Memory Aid (*Think of **R**BBB and the "**r**'s"*) — in that there is an **r**S**R**' complex with the taller *right* rabbit ear (the R') in a *right-sided* lead (i.e., V_1).

❖ *Typical LBBB*

The appearance of *typical* complete LBBB in the three *KEY* leads (I, V_1, and V_6) is schematically shown in the Figure below. Diagnostic criteria include:

- **QRS widening** to *at least* **0.12 second**.
- An **upright** (monophasic) **QRS** complex in **leads I** and **V_6**. The QRS may be notched— but there should *not* be any q wave in either lead I or lead V_6 !
- A *predominantly* **negative QRS** complex in **lead V_1**. There may or may not be an initial small r wave in lead V_1. (That is, lead V_1 may show *either* a *QS* or *rS* complex.).

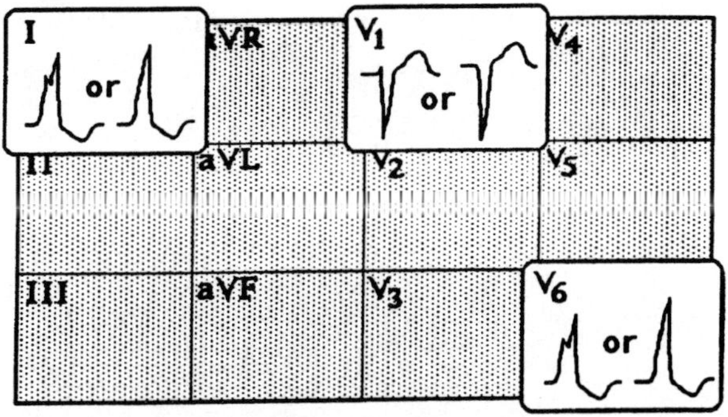

ECG appearance of the QRS complex in the 3 *KEY* leads with *typical* **complete LBBB**. Note that there should *never* normally be a Q wave in a left-sided lead (I, V_6) with typical LBBB. (Finding a Q in I, aVL, or V_6 suggests that the patient has had an infarction at some point in the past.)

❖ IVCD (<u>I</u>*ntra*<u>V</u>*entricular* <u>C</u>*onduction* <u>D</u>*elay*)

The ECG appearance of IVCD is difficult to characterize. This is because IVCD is often the ***end result*** of a number of *different* pathophysiologic processes— rather than reflecting a discrete defect in the conduction system (as usually occurs with RBBB or LBBB). Examples of conditions that may lead to IVCD include myocardial infarction, cardiomyopathy with ventricular fibrosis, chamber enlargement— and/or any *combination* of these (*with or without* a component of bundle branch block). Thus, many patients with IVCD have at least *some type* of underlying heart disease. According to the algorithm on page 21— **IVCD** is present <u>IF</u>:

- The **QRS complex** is ***wide*** (i.e., ≥0.11 second).
    - *Neither* **typical RBBB** *nor* **typical LBBB** is present.

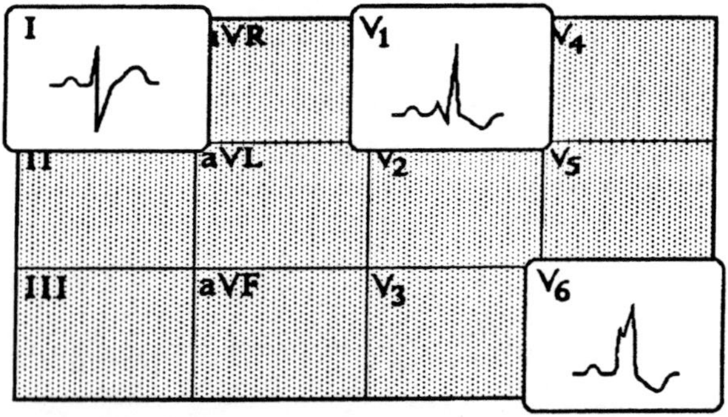

Schematic example of **IVCD** in that there is sinus rhythm and QRS widening— but QRS morphology is *not* typical for either RBBB or LBBB in *all* 3 of the *KEY* leads (i.e., leads I and V_1 are consistent with RBBB— but lead V_6 suggests LBBB!).

Typical *Secondary* ST-T Wave Changes

RBBB and LBBB each alter the *sequence* of ventricular depolarization. This is why they produce the alterations in QRS morphology that we have just discussed. As a *direct* result of this altered sequence of activation— these conduction defects *also* alter the sequence of ventricular *repolarization*, which leads to development of ***secondary*** **(2°) ST-T wave changes** (*See Figure below*). These ST-T wave changes are called secondary— because they are the direct *result* of (i.e., they are *secondary* to) the conduction defect itself.

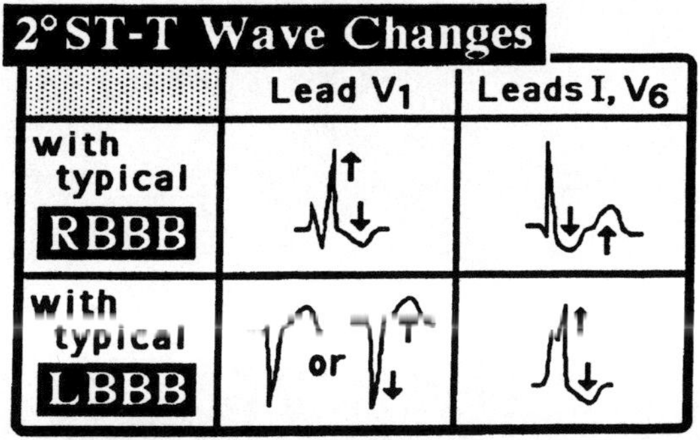

❖ **KEY Rule-** As in the Figure, the ST segment *and* T wave should normally be oriented ***opposite*** to the ***last*** **QRS deflection** (*arrows*) in the 3 *KEY* leads when there is *typical* RBBB or LBBB. Deviation from this pattern in *any* of the 3 *KEY* leads is abnormal, and indicates a ***primary*** **(1°) ST-T wave change**— suggesting that ischemia or infarction *may* be occurring.

"*RBBB-Equivalent*" Patterns (in lead V_1)

The shape of the QRS complex in lead V_1 may vary greatly with RBBB. It will *not* always show a "neat" rSR' (or rsR') in this lead. Instead, *any* of the patterns below (*See Figure*) qualify for the diagnosis of **RBBB**— as long as the QRS is *widened* (to ≥ 0.11 second) — *and* a wide *terminal* S wave is present in left-sided leads (I and V_6).

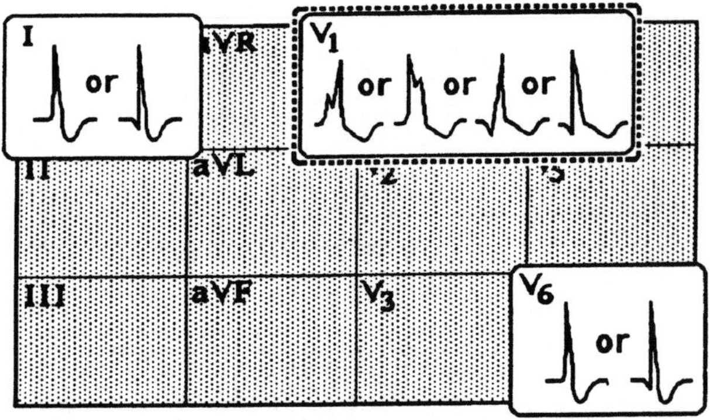

- **Diagnosis** of **Infarction** with **BBB**— is difficult, but *not* necessarily impossible! Look for 1° ST-T wave changes (*page 25*) — or *new* Q waves in *left-sided* leads (I, aVL, V_6) with LBBB. Evidence of infarction (Q waves, ST-T changes) is easier to see with RBBB.

- **Diagnosis** of **LVH** with **BBB**— Suspect LVH with LBBB if there is LAA *and/or* very *deep* S waves (≥30 mm) in V_1, V_2 or V_3; LVH is probably present with RBBB if the R in aVL ≥12 *and/or* R in V_5 or V_6 ≥25 (*page 37*).

WPW

In the setting of normal sinus rhythm— the *only* exception to the simplified algorithm presented on page 21 (for assessment of QRS widening) is the ***W**olff-**P**arkinson-**W**hite* (***WPW***) **syndrome**. Although admittedly uncommon (with an estimated incidence of 2 per 1,000 in the general population) — WPW occurs just often enough to cause problems for the unwary (principally by its role in facilitating reentry arrhythmias and *very rapid* A Fib).

The syndrome of WPW is recognized by the presence of *three* ECG findings: **1)** QRS widening; **2)** a ***delta*** wave; and **3)** a *short* PR interval. *Not all leads* necessarily show each of these findings. Thus, a ***delta* wave** is present in only *some* of the leads in the Figure below (*arrows*). When negative (as below in leads II, III, aVF) — the delta looks like a Q wave (and may simulate infarction). Note the tall R wave complex in lead V_1 (that simulates RBBB). This is why WPW is known as *"the great mimic"* !

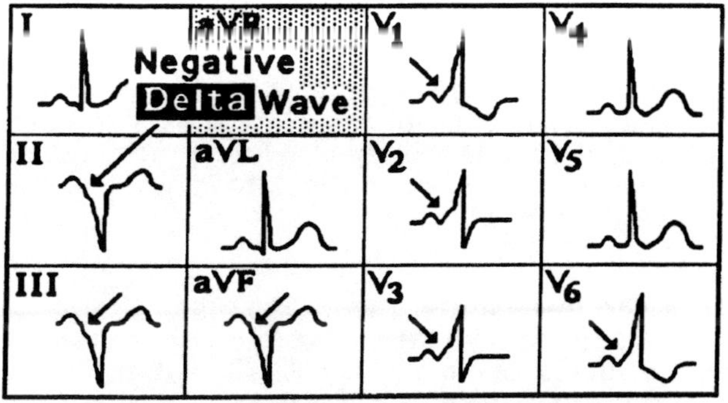

The QT Interval

The ***QT interval*** is the period that extends from the *beginning* of ventricular depolarization— until the *end* of ventricular repolarization (*See Figures below*). For practical purposes— the QT interval is ***prolonged*** if it clearly measures ***more*** than **half** the R-R interval. The principal exception to this general rule occurs when the heart rate is rapid (i.e., *more* than 100 beats/minute, or so) — in which case measurement of the QT interval has little clinical significance.

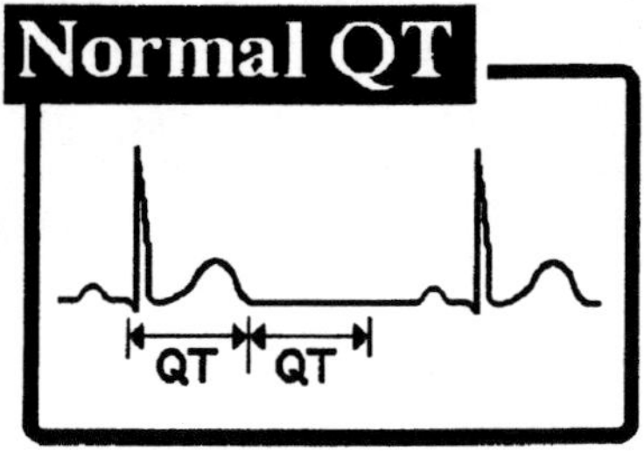

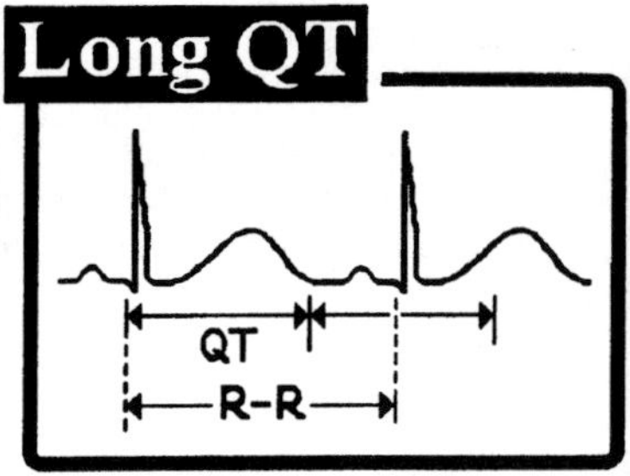

Determining **QT prolongation**. The QT interval is clearly normal on the left (since the QT is much *less* than half the R-R interval). In contrast— the QT is obviously *prolonged* on the right (since it far *exceeds* half the R-R interval).

<u>**KEY Clinical Point**</u>- Practically speaking— one *only* cares if the QT interval is normal or prolonged. (*Hypercalcemia* produces QT shortening— but this is very difficult to recognize clinically.)

The QT Interval: *KEY Points*

i) The QT interval is measured from the *onset* of the Q wave (or the onset of the R wave if there is no Q) — until the *termination* of the T wave.
ii) Select a lead in which you can *clearly* see the terminal boundary of the T wave. Select that lead in which the QT interval appears to be *longest*.
iii) Precise measurement of the QT interval is usually *not* necessary. Practically speaking— one only cares if the QT interval is normal or prolonged.
iv) Determination of the QT interval means little when the heart rate is rapid (*faster* than ≈90-100/minute).

Common Causes of ***QT Prolongation***

- ***Drugs***— Type 1A (i.e., quinidine, procainamide, disopyramide) and III (sotalol, dofetilide, amiodarone) antiarrhythmic agents
  — Tricyclic antidepressants/phenothiazines
- ***"Lytes"***— Hypokalemia (or hypomagnesemia),
  — Hypocalcemia
- ***CNS***— CNS catastrophes (i.e., stroke, seizure, coma, intracerebral or brainstem bleeding)

Note— Several *other* conditions (i.e., bundle branch block, infarction, and ischemia) may *also* cause QT prolongation. However, the presence of these ***other* conditions** will usually be *obvious* from inspection of the ECG.

Axis (and Hemiblocks)

A standard ECG is recorded by viewing the heart's electrical activity from 12 leads. Each lead records the heart's electrical potential from its own particular vantage point (*See Figure below*).

The three ***standard*** **limb leads** are I, II, and III— as derived from Einthoven's *equilateral* triangle. As a result — *each* of these leads is separated from each other by 60°, starting with **lead I** (at 0°) — followed by **lead II** (at +60°) and **lead III** (60° further away at +120°).

The ***augmented*** **limb leads** are each separated from each other by 120° — and as such form a *"Mercedes-Benz"* triangle (*dotted lines* in Figure) — beginning with *vertical* **lead aVF** (at +90°) — *lateral* **lead aVL** (at -30°) — and *distant* **lead aVR** (which we can usually *ignore*— and need *not* recall its degree location).

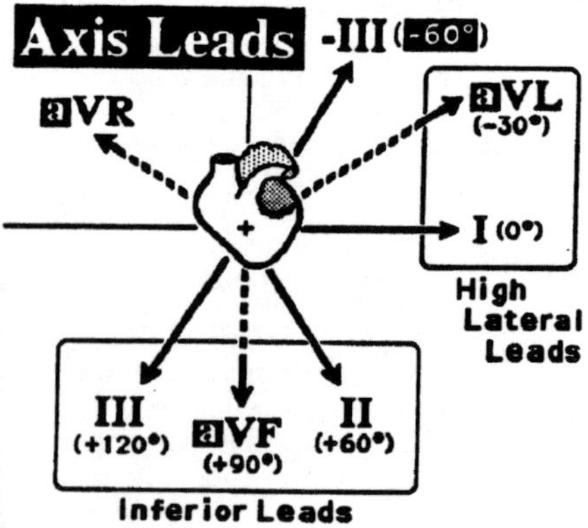

❖ **KEY Points:**

— Each of the limb leads (**I**, **II**, **III**) is *separated* by 60°.

— **Lead -III** is 60° *away* from lead I (in the *negative* direction at -60°).

— **Lead aVL** *bisects* lead I (at 0°) and lead -III (at -60°).

Calculation *of* ***Axis:*** Basic Principles

Mean QRS axis is calculated in the *frontal* plane. The **2 *KEY* leads** that are used for axis determination are **leads I** and **aVF**. Think of lead I as the *"starting"* point. As such, it is easy to remember that this *horizontal* lead is oriented toward 0° (*See Figure below*). Lead aV**F** is oriented *perpendicular* to lead I (i.e., looking *straight up* from the **F**eet). Lead aVF is therefore located 90° *away* from lead I, or at +90°.

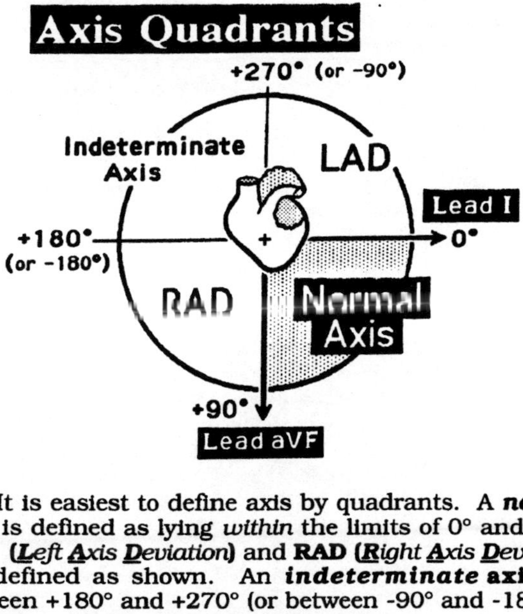

It is easiest to define axis by quadrants. A ***normal* axis** is defined as lying *within* the limits of 0° and +90°. **LAD** (*__L__eft __A__xis __D__eviation*) and **RAD** (*__R__ight __A__xis __D__eviation*) are defined as shown. An ***indeterminate* axis** lies between +180° and +270° (or between -90° and -180°) — depending on the observer's perspective.

Rapid Determination** of **Axis

Determination of the mean axis ***quadrant*** can be made *at a glance*— by inspection (and comparison) of the *net* QRS deflection in leads I and aVF:

Axis Determination

	Net QRS Deflection	
	Lead I	**Lead aVF**
Normal Axis	Positive	Positive
RAD	Negative	Positive
LAD	Positive	Negative
Indeterminate	Negative	Negative

- If the approximate size (i.e., *net* QRS deflection) of lead I is about the same as that for lead aVF— then the mean QRS axis should lie *midway* between these leads (or close to +45°). We often provide a *range* for our answer (i.e., *"The axis lies between +40° and +50°"*).
- If the *net* QRS deflection of lead I is positive and clearly *exceeds* that for lead aVF— then the mean QRS axis lies *closer* to lead I (i.e., *between* 0° and +40°).
- The axis lies *closer* to lead aVF (i.e., *between* +50° and +90°) — if the *net* deflection in aVF is greater.
- The axis is *perpendicular* to (i.e., **90° away** from) a lead where the QRS complex is ***isoelectric*** (equal parts positive and negative).
- **All you are doing** is ***approximating.*** Axis calculation need <u>not</u> be exact— *as long as you are in the "ballpark"* (that is, *within* about 20-30°, or so) !!!

Pathologic **LAD** (Left Axis Deviation)

__L__eft __A__nterior __H__emi__B__lock (**LAHB**) is far more common than *__L__eft __P__osterior __H__emi__B__lock* (**LPHB**). This is because the left posterior hemifascicle is much thicker than the anterior hemifascicle. It also has a dual blood supply (from the left and right coronary arteries) — whereas the anterior hemifascicle does not.

For practical purposes, we equate the ECG diagnosis of LAHB with the finding of ***pathologic* LAD**, which we define as a mean QRS axis *more negative* than -30°.

> ❖ ***__KEY__* __Point__—** One need *only* look at **lead II** to make the diagnosis of *pathologic* LAD. __IF__ the *net* QRS deflection in lead II is more ***negative*** than positive— then the mean QRS axis *must* be more negative than -30° (which means there is **LAHB**) !

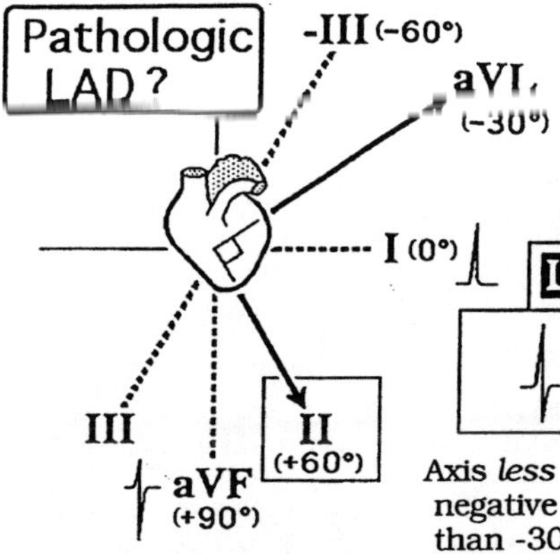

❖ If there is **LAD** (as determined by the presence of a *positive* deflection in lead I and a net *negative* deflection in lead aVF) — *Look next* at **lead II**:

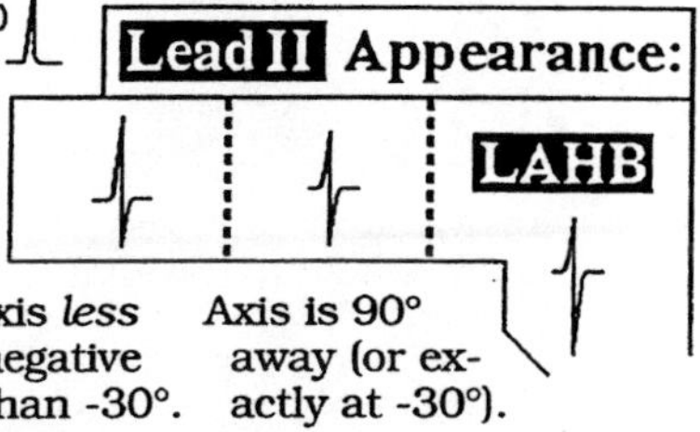

Recognition *of the* ***Hemiblocks***

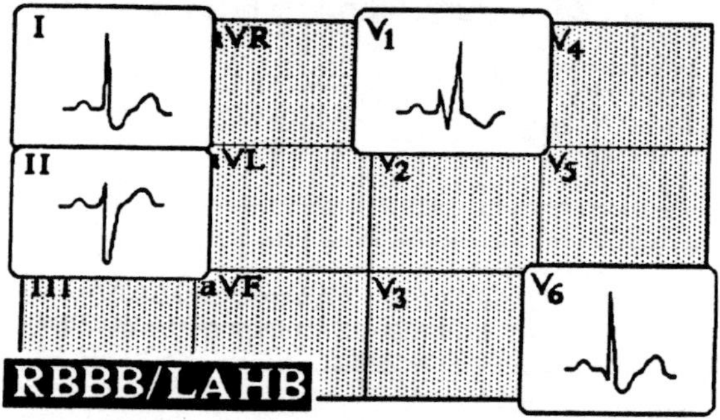

There is ***bifascicular* block**— in the form of RBBB and LAHB. **LAHB** is diagnosed because the *net* QRS deflection in lead II is *negative* (*See page 33*).

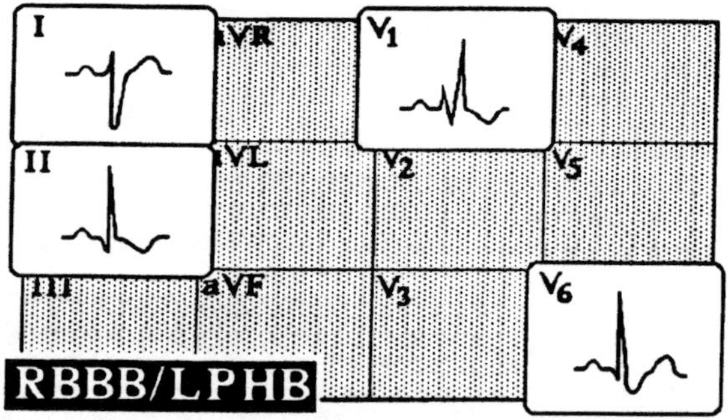

There is again ***bifascicular* block**— in this case from RBBB and **LPHB** (diagnosed by the finding of a very *deep* straight component to the S wave in lead I). Lead II (and also lead III) show the *opposite* configuration of lead I when there is LPHB (small q; tall R).

Chamber Enlargement

LVH — *Clinical* Detection

The unfortunate clinical reality is that the ECG is *not* very accurate as a diagnostic tool for determining chamber enlargement. Even in the best of hands— *sensitivity* for detecting ***LVH*** (***L****eft* ***V****entricular* ***H****ypertrophy*) does *not* exceed 60% (although *specificity* may approach 90 to 95% when certain criteria are met). Diagnostic accuracy for determining ***RVH*** (***R****ight* ***V****entricular* ***H****ypertrophy*) and atrial enlargement is even less. (Echocardiography is far superior to the ECG for diagnosing enlargement of *any* cardiac chamber.)

Simplified **Criteria** for Diagnosing **LVH**

1. Deepest S wave in lead V_1 *or* V_2,
   plus tallest R wave in lead V_5 *or* V_6 ≥ **35**.

   — *and/or* — R in lead aVL ≥**12**.

2. Patient ≥ **35** years old.
3. Left ventricular (LV) "***strain***".

For adults 35 or over— remembering the numbers **35** and **12** allows diagnosis of LVH *most* of the time when it is possible to do so by 12-lead ECG. Only *one* of these criteria (35 *or* 12) need be met to diagnose LVH. These criteria are *not* valid for younger patients (under 35). If "***strain***" is present *in addition to* voltage— the specificity (accuracy) for *true* LVH is greatly increased.

❖ **Additional Voltage Criteria**- may occasionally be needed to diagnose LVH. We favor *any* of the following:

— An R wave ≥20 in *any* inferior lead (II, III, or aVF).
— A *deep* S wave (≥20-25) in lead V_1 or lead V_2.
— A *tall* R wave (≥25) in lead V_5.
— A *tall* R wave (≥20) in lead V_6.

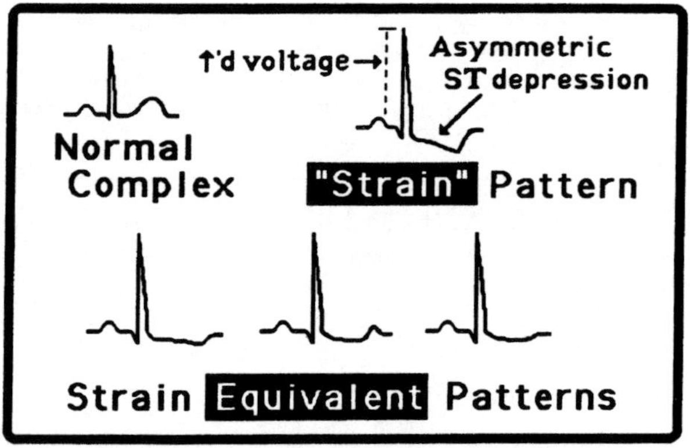

❖ **"Strain"**— is a pattern of *asymmetric* ST segment depression and T wave inversion (*See Figure*). LV strain is most commonly seen in one or more leads that look at the *left* ventricle (leads **I**, **aVL**, V_4, $\mathbf{V_5}$, $\mathbf{V_6}$); less commonly it can be seen in inferior leads.

Note— If a ***strain*** **equivalent** pattern (*See above*) occurs in association with *voltage* for LVH— this finding greatly increases specificity for *true* LVH compared to voltage criteria alone.

❖ **<u>What if there is a Conduction Defect?</u>** (*See page 26*)

- Suspect LVH *despite* RBBB- <u>IF</u> the R in aVL is ≥12, or the R wave in V_5 or V_6 is ≥25.
- Suspect LVH *despite* LBBB or IVCD- <u>IF</u> the S wave in V_1, V_2, or V_3 is very deep (≥30).
- It is probably best *not to even bother* trying to diagnose RVH when LBBB, RBBB, or IVCD is present.

Atrial Abnormality (P Wave Appearance- *See Figure*)

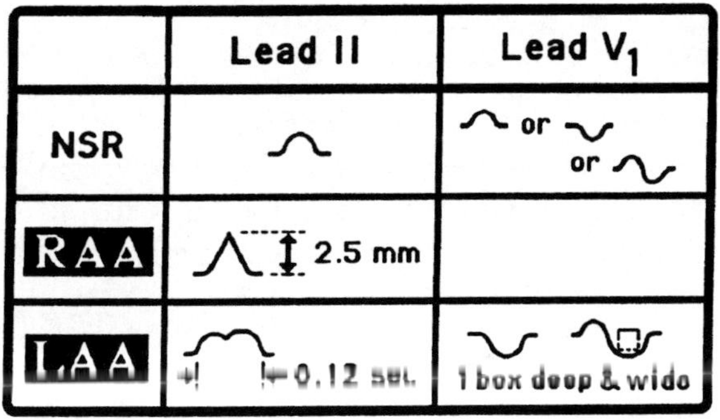

- **NSR (*<u>N</u>ormal <u>S</u>inus <u>R</u>hythm*)**— The P wave should normally be *upright* in lead II if there is NSR. The P may *normally* be positive, negative, or *biphasic* in lead V_1.
- **RAA (*<u>R</u>ight <u>A</u>trial <u>A</u>bnormality*)**— is diagnosed by the finding of tall ***<u>P</u>eaked*** and ***<u>P</u>ointed*** P waves in the ***<u>P</u>ulmonary*** leads (II, III, aVF). If the P wave looks "uncomfortable to sit on"— *think RAA!* = **<u>P</u>** **<u>P</u>**ulmonale.
- **LAA (*<u>L</u>eft <u>A</u>trial <u>A</u>bnormality*)**— is diagnosed by finding an **<u>m</u>**-shaped (*notched*) and *widened* P wave (≥0.12 second) in a "**<u>m</u>**itral" lead (I, II, aVL) — *and/or* a deep *negative* component to the P in lead V_1 = **<u>P</u>** **<u>M</u>**itrale.

ECG Diagnosis of RVH

Detection of right ventricular enlargement in adults by ECG criteria is often exceedingly difficult. This is because the left ventricle is normally so much larger and thicker than the right ventricle in adults— that it masks even moderate increases in right ventricular chamber size. As a result, many patients with RVH *won't* be identified if assessment for chamber enlargement is limited to obtaining an ECG.

Think of the ECG diagnosis of RVH as similar to making a ***"detective" diagnosis***. Rarely will any one finding clinch the diagnosis. Instead— determination of RVH is most often made by deduction (i.e., from identifying a *combination* of the following ECG findings):

Findings *Suggestive* of **RVH** in Adults:

1. RAD or *indeterminate* axis.
2. RAA (which very often accompanies RVH).
3. Incomplete RBBB (or an rSr' in lead V_1).
4. Low voltage (especially if emphysema present).
5. Persistent precordial S waves.
6. *"Strain"* in right ventricular leads.
7. Tall R wave in lead V_1.

❖ **KEY Points**- *None* of the criteria listed above *by itself* is enough to make the diagnosis of RVH. However, the presence of *several* of these criteria (when seen together on a single tracing) is *very* suggestive of RVH— especially when they occur in a likely setting (i.e., in a patient with COPD, right-sided heart failure, pulmonary hypertension *and/or* pulmonary stenosis). — *See Figure on page 39* —

❖ **<u>Example</u>** of **<u>RVH</u>**- Most of the ECG criteria for **RVH** are present in the tracing shown below (RAD, RAA, tall R in V_1, deep S waves in V_5, V_6). Note also that there is ***"RV strain"*** (which is typically seen in inferior *and/or* anterior leads— *both* of which are present here).

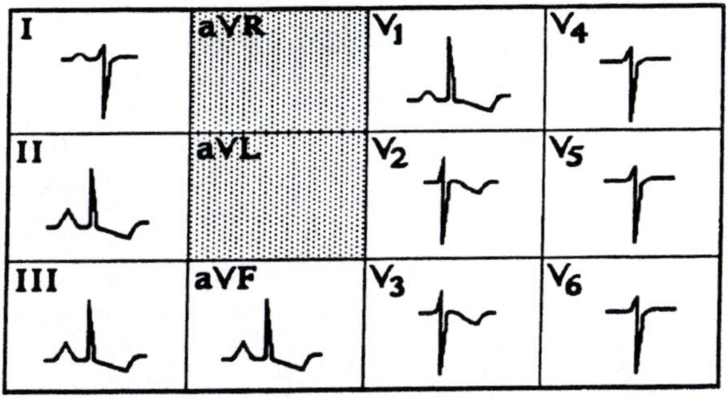

❖ **<u>Pulmonary Disease</u>** (such as **COPD**) may sometimes be suggested by ECG— <u>IF</u> at least *two* of the first 5 findings noted on page 38 are seen (*See Figure below*).

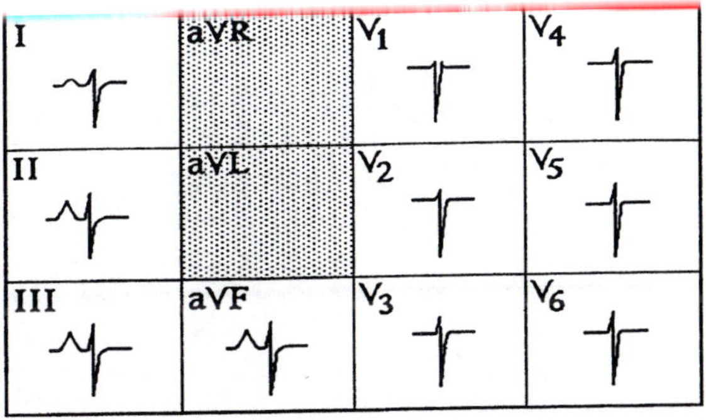

❖ **Pulmonary Embolism**- is most often associated with sinus tachycardia and/or non-specific ST-T wave changes. The ECG is usually *not* diagnostic— although sudden development of A Fib *and/or* ECG findings of **acute *right* heart "strain"** (which entails similar findings as RVH- *See page 38*) may suggest this diagnosis.

LVH Summary: *Which Leads for What?*

- **LV "strain"**— which is usually seen in *at least* one of the following leads: I, aVL, V_4, V_5, *and/or* V_6.
- **Atrial Abnormality**— the *two* leads to look at for detecting LAA (or RAA) are leads II and V_1 (*arrows*).
- **Voltage** for **LVH**— Use the leads *within* the heavy line below (= *deepest* S in V_1,V_2 — plus the *tallest* R in V_5,V_6) — or use the R wave in lead aVL (*dotted* box) — with **35** and **12** as the *KEYs* (*See page 35*).

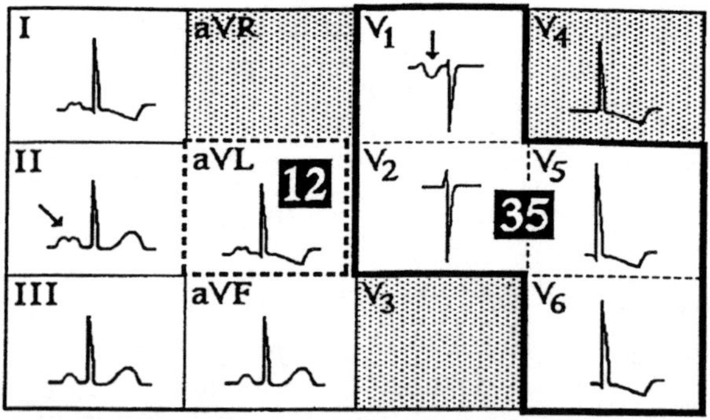

QRST Changes

The "heart" of ECG interpretation resides with assessing the tracing for ***QRST* Changes**. The purpose of this mnemonic— ***Q - R - S - T*** —is to ensure a systematic approach— *so that nothing is left out.* The most common mistake that occurs when a systematic approach is *not* closely followed is to allow more dramatic ST segment and T wave changes to consume one's attention— while subtler (but *equally* important findings) go unnoticed. Examples of such *all-too-easy-to-overlook* findings include recognition of a dominant R wave in lead V_1 and poor R wave progression. Routine adherence to a ***systematic* approach** *not* only prevents such findings from being overlooked— but ends up *saving time* in the long run.

Assessing for ***Q - R - S - T*** Changes

1. *Ignore* lead aVR.
2. Scan *each* of the other 11 leads for **Q waves**.
   Note the leads in which Q waves are found.
3. Check for **R wave progression**:
   - Does *transition* occur in the usual place?
   - Is there a *Tall R wave* (or rSr') in *lead* V_1 ?
4. Look at all leads (*except* aVR) for:
   - Changes in the **ST segment** (i.e., elevation or depression) — *and/or* changes in the **T wave**.

Precordial Lead Appearance

The Figure below shows a schematic cross-sectional view of the heart— in which ***arrows*** depict the general direction of **LV** (*left* ventricular) depolarization. The smaller **RV** (right ventricle) predominantly sees electrical activity as moving *away* from the right (and *toward* the larger and thicker left ventricle). This accounts for the fact that in a normal ECG ***right-sided*** **precordial leads** (V_1 and V_2) are predominantly negative— whereas ***left-sided*** **leads** (V_5 and V_6) are predominantly positive. The area where the R wave *becomes* greater than the S wave (***transition***) occurs normally in this Figure (i.e., *between* V_2 to V_4).

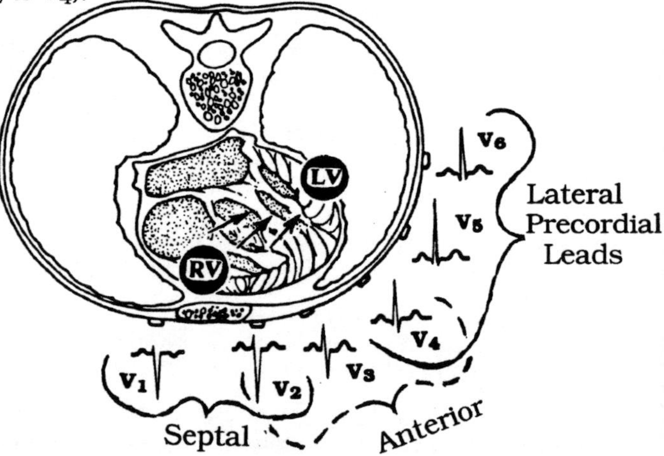

Note the *overlap* between leads viewing the *septal*— *anterior*— and *lateral* precordial areas.

The ***Basic* Lead Groups** (*See page 30*):

- Inferior leads- II, III, aVF
- Septal leads- V_1, V_2
- Anterior leads- V_2 to V_4
- Lateral (*left-sided*) leads:
  - Lateral precordial leads- V_4 to V_6
  - High lateral leads- I, aVL

R Wave Progression

Normally the R wave becomes *progressively* taller as one moves across the precordial leads (*See QRS complexes in Figure on page 42*). A number of conditions may be associated with ***"poor"*** **R wave progression**— in which the R wave in leads V_1 through V_3-V_4 either does *not* become bigger, or only increases very slowly in size:

Causes of ***P**oor* **R** **W**ave **P**rogression (***PRWP***):

- LVH
- RVH
- Pulmonary disease (i.e., COPD, chronic asthma)
- Anterior or anteroseptal infarction
- Conduction defects (i.e., LBBB, LAHB, IVCD)
- Cardiomyopathy
- Chest wall deformity
- Normal variant
- Lead misplacement

❖ **Examples** of **PRWP**- The patient below has **COPD** (suggested by RAD, RAA, persistent precordial S waves).

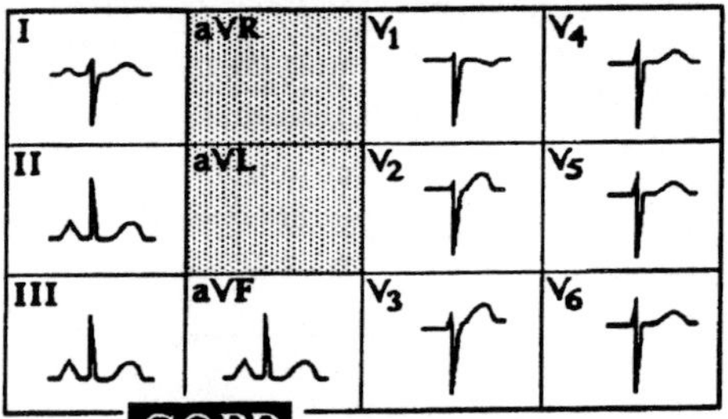

COPD -See Page 39-

Despite the PRWP— anterior infarction is *less* likely in this tracing because an r wave *is* present in *all* precordial leads (albeit the r wave is small).

Shown below (left) is *PRWP* from ***anteroseptal infarction*** (suggested by the complete *lack* of any r wave at all in leads V_1, V_2, *and* V_3). One *can't* be nearly as sure about infarction on the right because a small r wave *does* develop by lead V_3 (*We'd say 'possible' anteroseptal infarction* . . .). Statistically, realize that finding a **QS** in **leads V_1-V_2** is more likely *not* to be due to infarction.

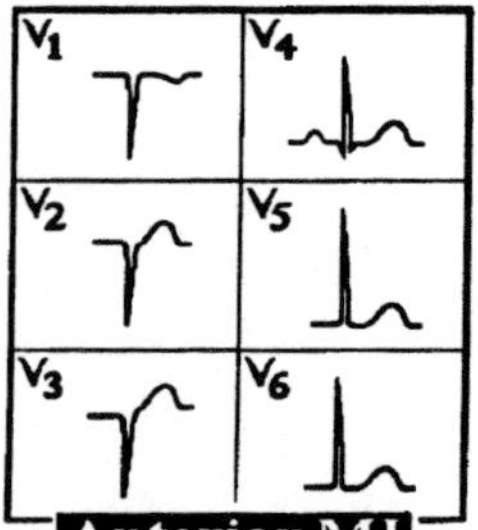

Anterior MI

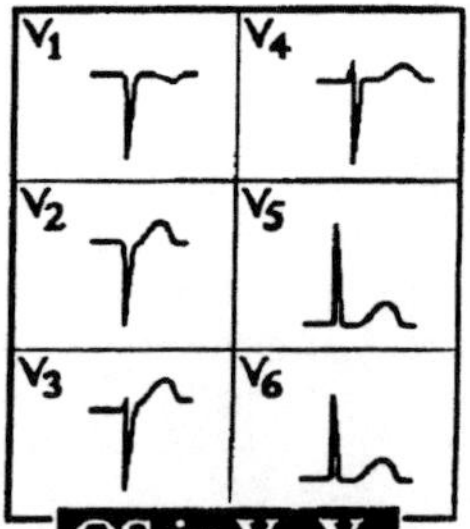

QS in V_1, V_2

Q Waves/T Wave Inversion— a *Normal* Finding

Several leads may *normally* display moderate-to-large size **Q waves** *and/or* **T wave inversion** (*See Figure*).

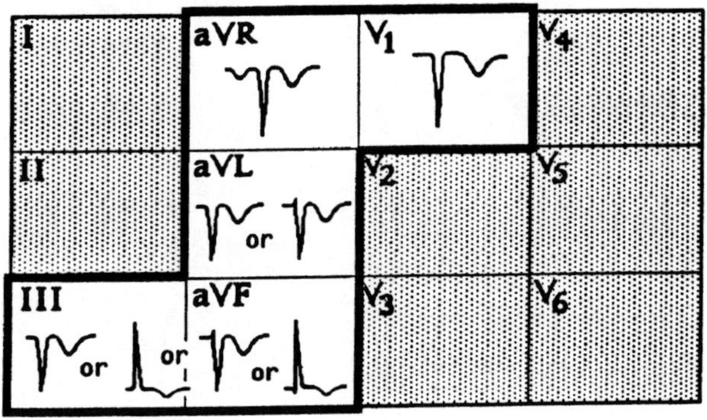

— Leads **III** — **aVF** — **aVL** — **aVR** — and **V1** —

- Note #1- Small and narrow ***normal*** **septal q waves** will often be seen in one or more of the *lateral* leads (I, aVL, V4, V5, or V6) in asymptomatic individuals who do *not* have heart disease (*See inside back cover*).

- Note #2- In general we can ***ignore*** lead **aVR**— since it *rarely* contributes useful clinical information.

- Note #3- ***Isolated*** **T wave inversion** in lead **III**, **aVF**, or **aVL** (*as above*) is most likely not to reflect ischemia when the QRS is *also* negative in these leads.

The *Shape* of **ST Segment Elevation**

ST segment elevation with an *upward* concavity (i.e., ***"smiley"*** configuration) is usually benign— especially when seen in an otherwise healthy, asymptomatic individual (and when seen with *notching* of the J point in one or more leads). This is known as ***early*** **repolarization**.

In contrast, ST segment elevation with coving or a *downward* convexity (***"frowny"*** configuration) — is much more likely to be due to acute injury (from acute infarction).

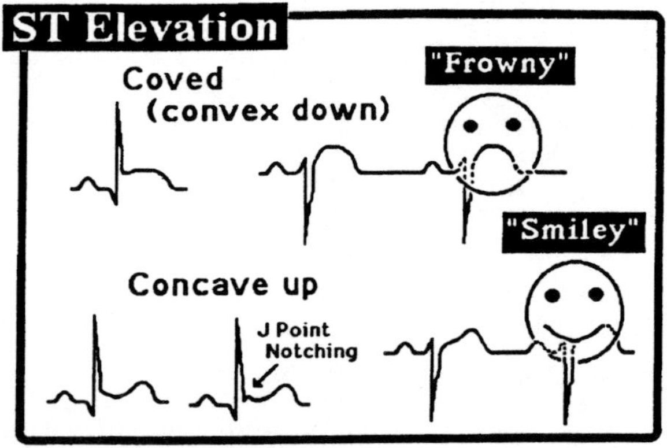

- ***KEY* Point**- History is *ever* important. Although ST elevation with a ***"smiley"*** configuration and J point ***notching*** often reflects a *normal* variant— this is *only* true IF the patient is *asymptomatic*. An *identical* ST pattern from a patient with chest pain *must* be assumed abnormal (and *possibly* indicative of acute infarction) until *proven* otherwise.

Common Causes of **ST Segment Depression**

1. Ischemia
2. "Strain"
3. Digitalis effect
4. Hypokalemia/Hypomagnesemia
5. Rate-related changes
6. Any *combination* of the above

The specific cause of ST segment depression in a given tracing may be suggested by the appearance of the ST segment and T wave itself (*See Figure below*). For example, ***"strain"*** (for LVH) is suggested by *asymmetric* ST depression in *lateral* leads— especially if voltage criteria (*on page 35*) are met. "RV strain" is suggested if the picture *below* is seen in *right-sided* leads in a patient with RVH (*pp 38-39*). **Ischemia** is suggested by *symmetric* T wave inversion— especially when seen in two or more leads of a group (i.e., in II, III, *and* aVF). Digoxin (**"Dig effect"**) may produce *either* ST "scooping" (*See below*) — or a "strain"-like pattern— or no change at all. Finally, there are **NS ST-T Abns** (*Non-Specific ST-T wave Abnormalities*) such as ST flattening or slight depression.

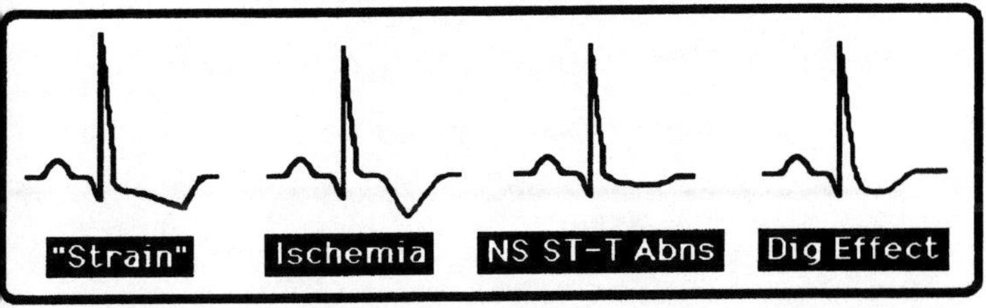

Infarction and **Ischemia**

One of the most important reasons for obtaining an ECG is to help evaluate the patient who presents with *new-onset* chest pain. By doing so we hope to determine:

1. If *any* ***acute*** **changes** are present.
2. If there is evidence of ***prior*** **infarction**.

Specifically— we want to determine if the patient being evaluated is *acutely* infarcting or ischemic. If so, what area of the heart is involved, how extensive is the involvement, are *other* abnormalities present (i.e., AV block, conduction defects, arrhythmias) — and most importantly, is the patient a candidate for acute intervention (i.e., with thrombolytic therapy or angioplasty) ?

> **KEY Points**- Be aware that as many as 1/3 of *all* infarcts are ***"silent"*** **MIs** (i.e., *not* associated with chest pain). Instead there may be dyspnea, mental status changes, or no symptoms at all. Use of a ***prior*** **ECG** may be *invaluable* for determining if abnormalities seen on a current tracing are new or old. To facilitate comparison—***fax*** tracings.

Acute Infarction: ***What are the Changes?***

There are 4 principal **ECG indicators** of acute infarction:

1. ST segment elevation
2. T wave inversion
3. Development of Q waves
4. *Reciprocal* ST segment depression.

ECG Changes with Acute MI Evolution

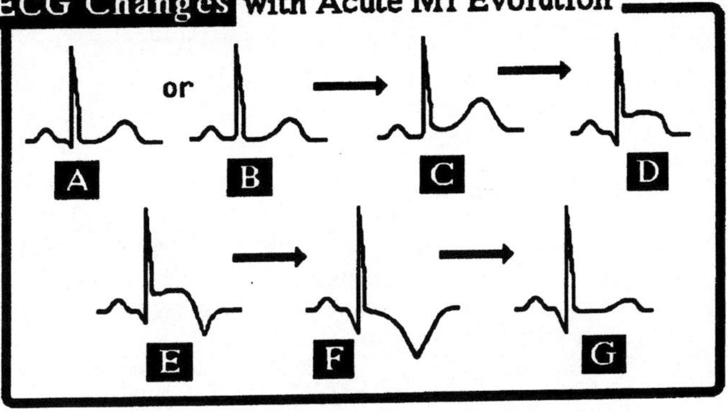

- **A** and **B** — show a normal QRS complex *before* any changes develop. Note that a small *narrow* q wave may often be present (as in **A**) as a *normal* finding (reflecting **normal *septal* q waves** that are commonly seen in lateral leads). Q waves of infarction tend to be bigger and wider.
- **C** — shows the "***hyperacute*** **stage**", which is the *earliest* change of Acute MI, in which the T wave becomes broader and peaks (almost as if "trying" to lift the ST segment). This change may be *subtle* (and easy to miss!); it usually is short-lived.
- **D** — Conventional ST elevation follows (with ST coving/"frowny" shape) — and developing Q waves.
- **E** and **F** — Q waves become bigger, ST elevation is maximal, and T wave inversion begins. T waves evolve as ST segments return to baseline (in **F**).
- **G** — ST-T wave abnormalities resolve (or nearly resolve) — but there is *persistence* of Q waves.

❖ *KEY* **Points** regarding the **ECG** with **Acute MI:**

- Not all patients with Acute MI develop ECG changes. As many as 1/3 do *not* develop changes— especially if MI occurs in electrically *silent* areas of the heart.
- The *A thru F* sequence (*on page 49*) represents the "typical" evolution of Acute MI. But— *many patients don't read the textbook!* Variations on this theme are common (i.e., ST depression or T wave inversion may be the *only* change, Q waves *don't* always develop, Q waves sometimes *resolve* with time, etc.).
- ***Non-Q wave* infarctions** may occur. These tend to be "incomplete" infarctions (often *not* transmural) — and pose a high risk for reinfarction (i.e., *"completing"* the infarct) ⇒ *Consider early revascularization* !
- Because ECG changes are *not* always seen with Acute MI, and serum markers (CK-MB, troponin) may initially be negative— a *KEY* determinant of whether or not to admit a patient with chest pain to the hospital *must* be the **history**. In general, if in doubt— *Admit the patient* to rule out Acute MI!
- Acute ECG changes may be *subtle* (as in the hyperacute stage- *page 49*). Look for ***reciprocal* changes** (ST depression in leads *not* showing ST elevation) to help determine if ECG findings are acute (*page 53*). Use the concept of ***"patterns of leads"***. For example, if uncertain about whether a Q wave or T wave inversion in lead **III** or **aVF** is *clinically* significant— look at the *other* inferior lead (which is **lead II**) to see if these changes are also present (*See page 45*).

Coronary Anatomy: *Relation to* Site *of* Infarct

The most common cause of Acute MI is sudden *total* occlusion of a major coronary artery.

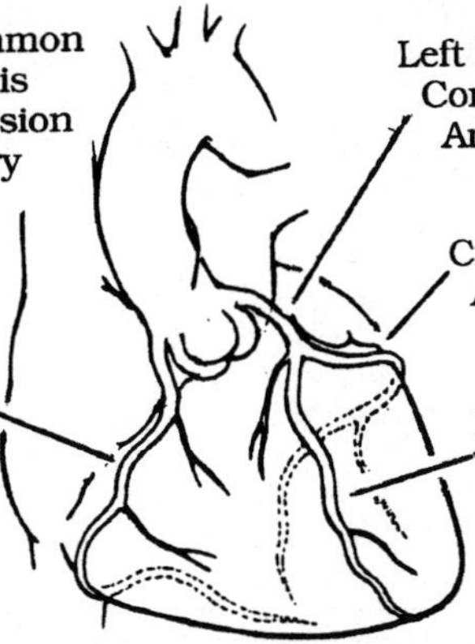

- Sudden total occlusion of the **RCA** (***R**ight **C**oronary **A**rtery*) causes acute *inferior* MI— and/or *posterior* or *right ventricular* MI. (ST elevation in **lead V_4R** helps diagnose RV infarction.) Mobitz I is common with inferior MI (the RCA supplies the AV nodal artery).
- Sudden occlusion of the **Left Main** coronary artery leads to sudden death (from massive infarction).
- Sudden occlusion of the **LAD** (***L**eft **A**nterior **D**escending*) artery leads to *anterior* infarction; bundle branch block/Mobitz II 2° AV block may be seen.
- Sudden occlusion of the **Circumflex** artery leads to *lateral* infarction. In about 10% of patients this artery (rather than the RCA) also supplies the inferior and posterior walls of the left ventricle.

Note— Collateral development *changes* the above patterns.

Treatment Goals:

Since the cause of Acute MI is most often sudden *total* occlusion of a major coronary artery— the goal of treatment should be to attempt to *restore* flow as soon as possible to the IRA (*Infarct-Related Artery*).

> **Note**- Acute angioplasty (with or without stenting) may be preferable IF available (*only* ≈20% of US hospitals have this on an emergency basis). As a result— thrombolytic therapy is the most commonly used method for attempting reperfusion.

Regarding *Thrombolytic* Therapy:

- ***Who Qualifies*** **?** — Ideally patients **<75 years old** with chest pain *and* **ST elevation** who are seen *less* than **6 hours** after symptom onset— and who have ***no* contraindications** to thrombolysis. (Criteria for thrombolysis have been expanded in *selected* cases to include *older* patients and those who are seen *more* than 6 hours after symptom onset.)

- ***Who Benefits Most?*** — Those seen ***earlier*** (ideally *within* 4 hours) — and those with ***larger* infarcts** (i.e., *anterior* location/*more* ST elevation with *more* reciprocal depression). Patients who have ***not yet* formed Q waves** (or with only *small* Q waves) are also more likely to benefit (greater chance of reversibility).

The *Mirror* Test/Tall R in Lead V_1

In the setting of acute *inferior* infarction— ST segment depression is commonly seen in the *anterior* leads (V_1, V_2, and V_3). There are **3** principal **causes** of this:

Causes of ***Anterior* ST Depression** in the Setting of Acute *Inferior* MI
1. Reciprocal changes* 2. Concomitant *anterior* ischemia* 3. Posterior infarction*
*Any *combination* of the above (*See* ***Figure*** *below*).

The Mirror Test

None of the standard precordial leads directly view the *posterior* wall of the left ventricle. ECG changes that occur in the posterior wall must therefore be inferred from *indirect* observation— which may be done by application of the Mirror Test. To do the test— ***Flip this page over***. Then *hold it up to the light!*

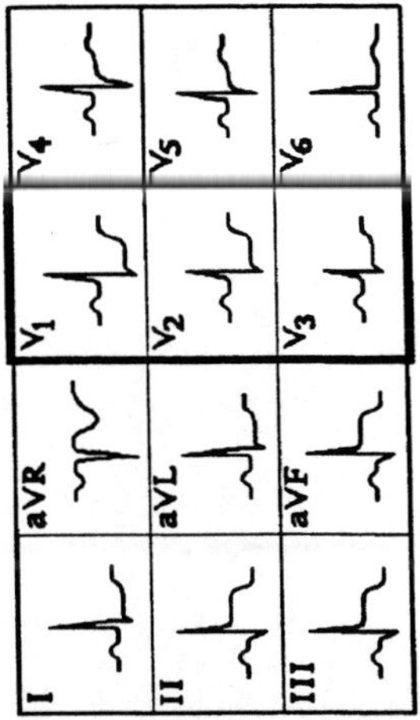

❖ **<u>Application</u>** of the ***<u>Mirror Test</u>***— Instructions are given *below.* The *anterior* precordial leads (V_1, V_2, V_3) provide a *mirror-image* view of the posterior wall of the left ventricle. Thus, the tall R waves and ST depression that is seen on page 53 (in V_1, V_2, V_3) — look like Q waves and coved ST elevation when the Mirror Test is done (*See Figure below*). Thus, the purpose of the Mirror Test is to facilitate recognition of ECG changes that *might* represent acute *posterior* MI.

<u>*Positive*</u> Mirror Test

Holding this page *up to the light* (and looking *through* it) — you should see a mirror image picture in *inverted* leads V_3, V_2, V_1 that looks

like this →

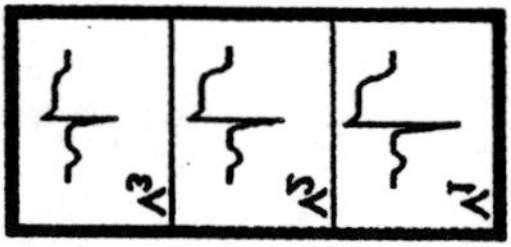

— and which is defined as a positive test.

The ***Tall R Wave*** in **Lead** V_1

Under normal circumstances, the QRS complex in lead V_1 is predominantly negative (*See page 42*). Finding a "***Tall***" **R wave** in **lead** V_1 (i.e., an R wave that *equals* or *exceeds* the S wave in this lead) is distinctly unusual— and should prompt consideration of the following:

Common Causes of a ***Tall R*** in **Lead** V_1

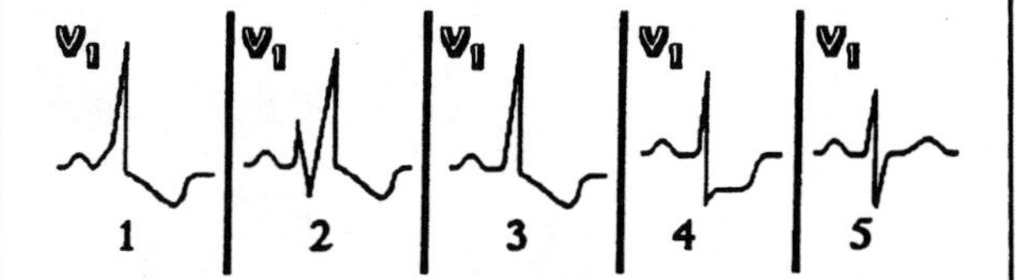

1. **WPW**— QRS widening/Short PR interval (*page 27*)
   - Delta waves (which may be positive or negative)
2. **RBBB**— QRS widening to ≥0.11 second (*page 22*)
   rSR' (or RBBB equivalent pattern) in lead V_1
   - Wide, terminal S wave in leads I and V_6
3. **RVH**— Normal QRS duration/RAA (*page 39*)
   - RAD or indeterminate axis/Low voltage
   - Persistent precordial S waves
   - Right ventricular strain
4. **Posterior Infarction**— Normal QRS duration
   - Evidence of inferior infarction
   - Positive "mirror test" (*pp 53-54*)
5. **Normal Variant**— Normal QRS duration
   - Diagnosed by ***exclusion*** (i.e., after *ruling out* WPW, RBBB, RVH, and posterior infarction)
   - Often found in otherwise healthy young adult

Electrolyte Disturbances

Hyperkalemia

An ECG should be obtained when electrolyte disturbance is suspected— especially for ***hyperkalemia*** (in which a fairly good correlation *does* exist between ECG findings and the serum potassium [K^+] level- *See Figure*).

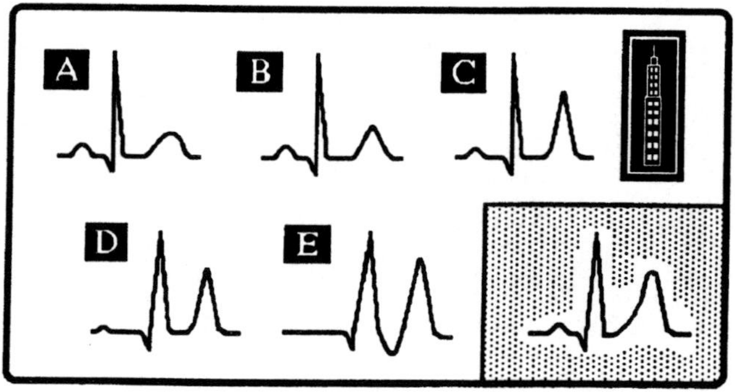

A — is normal. **B** — shows *peaking* of the T wave, which is the *earliest* change (K^+ ≈6-7 mEq/L). **C** — The T wave becomes *taller* and more peaked (K^+ ≈7-8 mEq/L); it almost looks like the ***empire state* building** (tall, peaked, with a *narrow* base) — in contrast to the T wave that is sometimes seen in healthy individuals as a ***normal* variant** (*shaded box*) — in which the T wave is rounded, its sides are *not* symmetric, and it has a *broad* base. **D** — P wave amplitude decreases, the PR interval lengthens, and the QRS widens (K^+ >8 mEq/L). **E** — P waves disappear (sinoventricular rhythm) and the QRS becomes sinusoid (K^+ >10 mEq/L). V Fib usually follows.

Hypokalemia

Although the ECG is a fairly good indicator of hyperkalemia— it is *not* reliable for detecting ***hypo-kalemia***. However, when ECG changes are seen— they tend to be those that are shown in the Figure below:

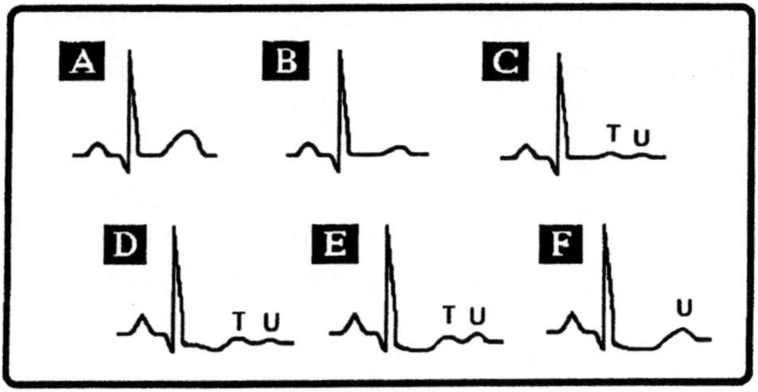

A — is normal. **B** — shows *flattening* of the T wave, which is the *earliest* change. **C** and **D** — A ***U wave*** then develops, associated with ST-T wave flattening and sometimes slight ST depression. A "pseudo P pulmonale" pattern may be seen. **E** and **F** — ST depression is more noticeable and the U wave increases in amplitude— until ultimately the U wave *overtakes* the T wave. At this point distinguishing between the T wave and U wave may be almost impossible ("Q-U" prolongation— as in **F**).

- **Note**- The ECG changes of ***hypomagnesemia*** are *identical* to those of hypokalemia. Hypomagnesemia is often seen in association with *other* electrolyte abnormalities (low sodium, potassium, calcium, or phosphorus); acute MI; cardiac arrest; digoxin or diuretic therapy; alcohol abuse, renal impairment.

Pericarditis

Pericarditis is often a difficult clinical entity to detect. Recognition of ***acute*** **pericarditis** can be facilitated by thinking of diagnosis as a 3 part process:

i) **History**— inquire about preceding *viral* illness.

ii) **Physical exam**— hearing a *pericardial* **friction *rub*** is the *most* diagnostic sign!

iii) **ECG findings**. These are divided into **4 stages**. The easiest way to remember these *sequential* changes is to conceptualize the four stages as follows:

- **Stage I** — everything is *UP* (i.e., ST elevation in *almost* all leads— *See page 59*).
- **Stage II** — transition (= *"pseudonormalization"*).
- **Stage III** — everything is *DOWN* (inverted T waves).
- **Stage IV** — normalization.

Stages of Pericarditis

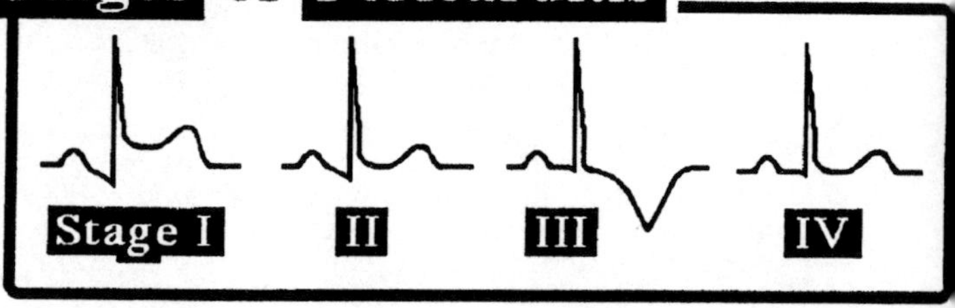

❖ **Stage I** of ***acute* pericarditis** is shown below. Note how diffuse ST segment elevation is in Stage I (*everything up"* stage) — being seen in virtually *all* leads *except* those "far away" (*shaded* leads aVR, V_1, III).

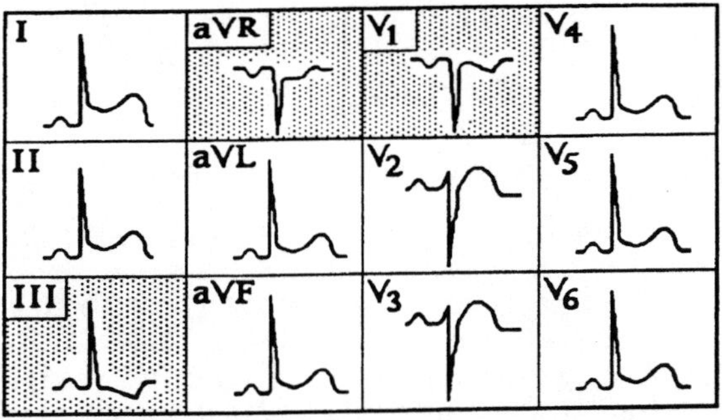

Distinction between the ST elevation of Stage 1 pericarditis— and that which is seen in early repolarization and acute MI can *usually* be made because:

- **Early repolarization** — is most often seen in otherwise *healthy* young adults. ST elevation is usually *localized* to one (or at most two) areas of the heart (*page 46*).

- ***Acute* MI**— is usually suggested by the history (older patient with risk factors; chest pain more constant and severe). The ECG may show Q waves, *reciprocal* ST depression and T wave inversion *while* the ST segment is *still* elevated— whereas with pericarditis the T wave typically does *not* invert until *after* the ST segment has returned to the baseline (*See Figure at right*).

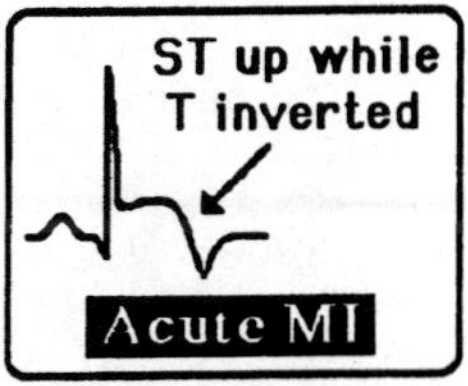

Applying the ***Systematic*** **Approach**

❖ **R A**te— Divide 300 by the number of boxes in the R-R Interval (*pg 5*).

❖ **R H**ythm— Are there P waves? Are P waves "married" to the QRS? (*pg 4*). **P waves** should *always* be ***upright*** in **lead II** if there is sinus rhythm (*unless* there is lead reversal or dextrocardia) — *Watch your* ***P's*** *&* ***Q's*** *— and the* ***3 R's*** *—*

❖ **I** ntervals— Be sure to look at intervals *early* in the process!

- The **PR Interval** (*pg 19*) — is *prolonged* IF >0.20-0.21 second (if clearly *more* than a *LARGE* box in duration).
- The **QRS Complex** (*pg 20*) — is *wide* IF >0.10 sec. (if *more* than *HALF* a *large* box).
- The **QT Interval** (*pg 28*) — is *prolonged* IF clearly *more* than *half* the R-R interval (provided that heart rate is *not more* than 100 beats/minute).

> ***KEY* Point**- If the QRS complex is wide, ***STOP*** and find out why (i.e., RBBB, LBBB, IVCD, or WPW) — *before* proceding further (*See pg 20*).

❖ **A** xis (*pg 31*)- is determined by looking at **lead I** (at 0°) and **lead aVF** (at +90°):

- The axis is ***normal***— IF *net* QRS deflection is *positive* in leads I and aVF.
- There is **RAD**— IF *net* QRS deflection is negative in I, but positive in aVF.
- There is **LAD**- IF the *net* QRS is positive in I, but negative in aVF. There is *pathologic LAD* (= **LAHB**- *See pg 33*) — IF *net* QRS is more *negative* than positive in lead II).
- The axis is ***indeterminate***— if *net* QRS deflection is *negative* in I *and* aVF.